"Feisty, literate, and uncompromising, the work of Kilstein and Kilkenny stresses the role of a free and independent press as a powerful guardian of democracy."

—*Publishers Weekly*

"[*Newsfail*] is one hell of a feisty, intelligent, and uncompromising read. This particular hybrid of memoir and truth-telling will make you rethink not only where you get your news, but how you get it, and what really matters when it comes to discussing the subjects humans *should* find vital to our existence."

—*Bustle*

"Kilstein and Kilkenny sound so damn smart and exude an aura of cool that you find yourself nodding along. . . . They intersperse funny, personal anecdotes among the serious and often downright depressing facts and figures. Between the pages of political agitation is a self-deprecating, snarky love story."

—*RedEye*

"[Kilstein and Kilkenny] make a strong case that a greater range of voices needs to be part of the national media discussion, including theirs. . . . A call to action for those who don't like the news to make their own."

—*Kirkus Reviews*

"Jamie Kilstein and Allison Kilkenny are a modern-day social justice, nonviolent, vegan, punk, antiwar, feminist Bonnie and Clyde. Their weapons are simple: the pen, the airwaves, and a searing sense of humor. Their targets are the rich, the powerful, corporate media barons, and basically any major-league assholes."

—Jeremy Scahill, Academy Award nominee and author of *Blackwater* and *Dirty Wars*

#NEWSFAIL

Climate Change, Feminism, Gun Control,
and Other Fun Stuff We Talk About
Because Nobody Else Will

Jamie Kilstein
and Allison Kilkenny

Simon & Schuster Paperbacks
New York   London   Toronto   Sydney   New Delhi

Simon & Schuster Paperbacks
An Imprint of Simon & Schuster, Inc.
1230 Avenue of the Americas
New York, NY 10020

First Simon & Schuster trade paperback edition October 2015

SIMON & SCHUSTER PAPERBACKS and colophon are registered trademarks of Simon & Schuster, Inc.

Graph on page 139 reprinted with permission of Danny Hayes/The Monkey Cage

For information about special discounts for bulk purchases,
please contact Simon & Schuster Special Sales at 1-866-506-1949 or
business@simonandschuster.com.

The Simon & Schuster Speakers Bureau can bring authors to your live event.
For more information or to book an event, contact the Simon & Schuster Speakers
Bureau at 1-866-248-3049 or visit our website at www.simonspeakers.com.

Interior design by Akasha Archer

Manufactured in the United States of America

10 9 8 7 6 5 4 3 2 1

The Library of Congress has cataloged the hardcover edition as follows:
Kilstein, Jamie.
  #Newsfail : how two godless vegans took on mainstream media so you don't have to /
Jamie Kilstein and Allison Kilkenny. — First Simon & Schuster hardcover edition.
    p. cm
1. Mass media—Political aspects—United States. 2. Political satire, American. 3.
Political culture—United States. 4. United States—Politics and government—Humor.
5. American wit and humor. I. Killkenny, Allison. II. Title. III. Title: Newsfail.
  P95.82.U6K55 2014
  302.23'0973—dc23

2014006887

ISBN 978-1-4767-0651-1
ISBN 978-1-4767-8341-3 (pbk)
ISBN 978-1-4767-0652-8 (ebook)

Thanks to . . .

Our families for humoring every: bad life decision, horrible career
path, anxiety-ridden phone call, and conversation that segued from
laughing to crying.

The *Citizen Radio* Maniacs, who make us feel less alone. And to the
CR family: Camille, Kevin, Sally, Hilary, and Jits.

Robin. Without your help, *CR* would not exist.

And Dangles . . . *Fuck* you, buddy. We wrote a book!

"The fools . . . THE FOOLS. Look at them. Foolish plebeians!
Burn! BURRRRRRNNNNNN!"

—Wolf Blitzer (probably)

CONTENTS

PREFACE

In Which the Authors Interview
Ralph Nader in the Bathtub

There were many points at which security could (and, in retrospect, *should*) have stopped us from entering MSNBC.

For starters, we are both covered in tattoos, neither of us possesses particularly sophisticated sartorial tastes, Allison sometimes has accidental "death stare," and Jamie often mistakes creepy for charming. We may have also had the wild-eyed, sweaty demeanor of newly liberated podcasters, recently escaped from an internet radio network that had asked us to take on Big Business sponsors—something we had strictly sworn off.

You see, the authors had aspirations of being pristine angels of independent media, untouched and unsullied by corporate cash. We would be the people's media—that was the whole idea behind the name of our show, *Citizen Radio*. There was also the fact that no sponsor in their right mind would touch our show, but phrasing it the first way made us feel better about ourselves.

That concept of being sponsor-free hadn't flown with the

people who, ya know, we were supposed to be making money for. Say, our former boss.

Our whole career up until that point had essentially been managers, agents, and other boss-types saying, "We love you because you are political and edgy!" Then, once they saw what that nightmare actually entails, added, "Hey, could you not be political or edgy? But everything else, we LOVE!"

Case in point: During a time when we were covering the NSA warrantless surveillance controversy, circa 2007, our former boss asked us to take on AT&T as a sponsor. Mind you, at the time AT&T was being sued over allegations that the company provided the NSA with its customers' phone and internet communications as part of a vast data-mining operation, so to us it seemed a *bit* like a conflict of interest.

"This is *Citizen Radio* saying, if you are going to be spied on, be spied on by the best: AT&T! They're *always* listening!"

That's when we decided to walk. We didn't need a network or bosses. We were going to be *free* and supported by our listeners! This was the first day of our triumphant escape from the milieu of servitude. No one would dictate what stories we could and could not cover. No one would censor us!

Freedom! Beautiful, terrible freedom!

The only problem was: no one knew us. No one knew what *Citizen Radio* was. Then, we had a brilliant idea. We would get some big names to appear on the podcast as guests to drive up traffic. Sure, no one knew who the hell Allison Kilkenny and Jamie Kilstein were, but have you heard of a little lady named *Rachel Maddow*? Huh?? Have you?!

That's what we thought.

Thus, in order to flee the belly of the beast, we found ourselves entering its lair. Corporateville. Sucktown. MSNBC. Mainstream media.

Sure, it was the liberal arm of the giant, but it was still the very thing we were trying to escape. This was sort of like if Code Pink hired General Petraeus as their PR person.

Regardless, Maddow was nice enough to invite us to a taping of her show and to sit down for an interview with us afterward.

NBC Studios at 30 Rock is located inside a beautiful building that was constructed to make you feel upon crossing its threshold like a failure who will never amount to anything. Or that's how we felt walking in, anyway. Everything is sleek surfaces and severe right angles. The carpet is printed with millions of small NBC peacocks, mocking your very existence. They seem to say, "Welcome to the real show, stupid podcasters!"

This was back in 2010, when MSNBC had recently granted Lawrence O'Donnell his own spot following Maddow. In fact, he was set to debut his show that very evening. Allison was dismayed at this news. From the first moment she laid eyes upon Mr. O'Donnell's face, Allison has always harbored a general mistrust of him. Maybe it was because of the MSNBC commercials where he's seemingly annexed a grade school classroom, occupied it, and refused to leave, and is now mansplaining life to his audience. Allison always imagined a class of third graders just out of frame, noses pressed to the door, their cries muffled as they plead, "Can we come back in yet, Mr. O'Donnell??"

Maddow's studio is a state-of-the-art thing of beauty. The three cameras that film the show are robotic and glide around the lacquered floor in an intricate ballet. For comparison, our current studio is located inside our apartment and our equipment comprises a laptop, microphones, and a blue kid's table from IKEA that cost twenty dollars. When we have a guest over, instead of having an unpaid intern who offers them a cappuccino, we have Jamie, who offers them a Zyrtec because "if the cats don't come in the office, they throw a real fit. This will help with the sneezing."

As an observer at MSNBC, you feel like a big clumsy ape in the robot cameras' presences, relocated to the side of the set on one of three chairs propped up on a platform, desperately trying not to do anything that will fuck up this awesome high-tech choreography.

Jamie glared angrily at the cameras. *Citizen Radio* is an extremely low-budget affair (remember: IKEA table), but was especially so in the early days, when we recorded the show on our cell phones. Both hosts (i.e., us) called into the same number and a soundboard on the internet would record the show. It's cool in the sense that anyone—literally, anyone—can create their own show, and we thought, *Hey! We're anyone! Let's make a pretend phone show!*

The only problem was, if the hosts stood too close together, there was massive feedback. This resulted in some highly awkward moments like when Allison and Jamie were interviewing then presidential candidate Ralph Nader, who was under the impression he was on a real show.

Nader gave a compelling answer to some question, and thrilled, Jamie flew back into the main room to give Allison an enthusiastic thumbs-up, which is when feedback tore through the room, and Allison whisper-shouted, "GET BACK IN THE BATHROOM!"

Jamie conducted the rest of the interview squatted in the bathtub and Mr. Nader probably realized he'd made a terrible mistake.

MSNBC doesn't have to deal with these kinds of problems. When Chris Matthews's earpiece goes out, he doesn't look over to Thomas Roberts, who is happily giving him the thumbs-up, and have to scream, "Back in the tub, Roberts!"

Jamie was having Nader-related flashbacks and was convinced he was going to somehow mess up *The Rachel Maddow Show*. The show is live and he has a track record of ruining quiet moments. Earlier that year, he accidentally pocket-dialed his brother during his family's Passover prayer. His family is still mad about that to this day. Seriously.

When you get on set at Maddow's show, guests are hooked into a sound pack so they can hear the whole show, including the video clips Maddow plays throughout the hour. The pack is fixed to the waistband of the guest's pants and a cord extends upward to an earpiece. Then the entire apparatus is attached to the chair. Other than the mouth-breather guests, the studio is virtually empty: just Rachel Maddow, a producer, and chairs.

Jamie did a frantic checklist. For example, he made sure his phone was off, so no one would hear his ringtone (*Glee*'s "Don't Stop Believing") during Maddow's Don't Ask, Don't Tell segment. And as if he wasn't stressed enough, now the authors were each strapped to a chair, perched atop a tiny ledge.

It's the worst place in the world to, say, have a spasming coughing fit. Unfortunately, that's exactly what happened to Allison, who desperately tried to remain quiet by muffling her distressed wheezing into her hand as though one of the robot cameras might come to life and attack her.

Jamie stared in shocked disbelief, not only trying to figure out what the hell to do, but also because it wasn't his fault! He wasn't the embarrassment! Allison was the responsible one. She's the one who drives to the emergency room, while Jamie is the one who asks, "How much blood can you lose before you die?!"

The harder she tried not to cough, the worse it got. Knowing she was about to experience an epic coughing fit, Allison darted off the platform, completely forgetting she was anchored to the chair. She would have torn it off the stage and fallen through the curtain had it not been for Jamie grabbing the chair as it flew past him. Allison quickly untangled herself from the sound pack, parted the curtains that led to the main floor of the studio, and nearly ran headfirst into . . .

Lawrence Fucking O'Donnell.

Allison almost clotheslined the guy set to debut his show that night, while projecting mucus all over his face, which in a weird way, is kind of a perfect metaphor for *Citizen Radio*. As cool as their elevators are, as nice as it would be to have a staff, or an office, or ROBOTS, it was clear this whole establishment-media thing and us would never work. Even when we're somehow accidentally on the inside, we always manage to fuck shit up.

INTRODUCTION

#NEWSFAIL: None of the News That's Fit to Print

The mainstream media has always been focused on sexy over substance, drama over facts—on what the scary Muslim next door might be plotting, which dishwashing liquid might kill you, or how the scary Muslim next door will use dishwashing liquid to kill you—while not reporting on what should *actually* be terrifying us. But their shallow coverage accelerated in 1996 when an insane Australian mogul named Rupert Murdoch bought Fox News Channel, a twenty-four-hour news station. Thus began not only Murdoch's foray into media empire construction, but also the birth of 'round-the-clock political propaganda channels masquerading as news.

Murdoch hired a frothing-at-the-mouth bulldog named Roger Ailes as Fox News's CEO and together they grew the network during the 1990s and 2000s to become the leading cable news network in the United States. Who could blame Americans for falling in love with Fox News? The hosts had SO MANY flag lapel pins!

During this time, forces on the left (the corporate left, anyway) decided to answer propaganda with . . . more propaganda! Starting in the mid-2000s, MSNBC, largely in response to the travesty of the US-led Iraq invasion, adopted an increasingly "progressive" stance later marketed as "Lean Forward" in a "we're in this together" ad campaign designed to elevate the network above its combative competitors.

But it was ironic that MSNBC adopted the progressive brand given that its behavior has been, and continues to be, extremely antiprogressive much of the time. Though it attempted to market itself as the network of the left, it quickly became clear MSNBC was more concerned with toeing the Democratic Party line than facilitating a space for purely liberal (or dare we hope, progressive) ideas.

Back in 2002, veteran talk show host Phil Donahue returned to TV with a show called *Donahue* on MSNBC. He did really well in the ratings, beating shows like *Hardball with Chris Matthews* and *Scarborough Country*, but Donahue was also a vocal critic of the Iraq invasion, and on February 25, 2003, MSNBC canceled the show, which probably doesn't sound very progressive to you. Unless maybe Donahue was a secret homophobic abortion protester?

Nope. Turns out, the *New York Times* intercepted an in-house memo in which a network executive complained: "Donahue represents a difficult public face for NBC in a time of war."[1] Fox News was crushing it in the ratings at the time by having blond women and 'roid-raging anchor dudes scream "AMERICA!!!" into the camera along with their camouflage-clad guests. On the "progressive network," Donahue was hosting thoughtful debates about the pros and cons of invading Iraq. That is, until they fired him.

This was by no means an isolated moment of partisanship.

When MSNBC anchor Ed Schultz had investigative journalist Jeremy Scahill on his show in 2011, Scahill pointed out that by putting boots on the ground in Libya, the United States would effectively be taking sides in a civil war. But what Schultz apparently heard was "DEATH TO AMERICA!" Here is the transcript:

> **Schultz:** I take President Obama's word for it, that troops will not be engaged on the ground. I take his word for it. Now, if he wants to hang me and my opinion out to dry as an American, that's fine.
>
> **Scahill:** Well, you know what? Your President Obama—
>
> **Schultz:** My President Obama?
>
> **Scahill:** He didn't call—
>
> **Schultz:** My President Obama? Is it your president, too? Jeremy, is he—wait a minute now. You're not going to beat to the water's edge. Is he your president, too?
>
> **Scahill:** Of course. I'm an American.
>
> **Schultz:** Okay.[2]

Here was a journalist speaking out against war, which in theory is supposed to be a democratic principle, but because we have a Democrat in the White House, Ed waged a live mini-McCarthy test on Jeremy, who we're pretty sure is not a Libyan spy.

And Ed wasn't alone among "progressive" news anchors in worshipping the president to the exclusion of any dissenting opinions. In a 2011 interview with *60 Minutes*, fellow MSNBC host Al Sharpton vowed never to criticize President Obama under *any circumstances*.

Sharpton told *60 Minutes* that if he finds fault with Obama, he'd be aiding those who want to destroy him. So Sharpton, a civil rights activist, has decided not to criticize the president about anything—even about black unemployment, which is twice the national rate.

Choosing not to criticize the president, even when he's wrong, even when he's doing very bad things, and instead lauding only the happy achievements of the administration, is not reporting the news—it's called peddling propaganda. It's like a football commentator refusing to acknowledge when his favorite team is playing badly. Only this time his bumbling team has the largest nuclear arms stockpile in the world and a fumble means the annihilation of the human species.

But listen, this isn't a book about journalistic objectivity, which in itself is a total myth. All journalists, reporters, and CEOs are biased. That's human nature. Even the authors of this book have biases! The only difference is, we're right. (Sorry.) But when networks stop engaging in journalism—which is more than reaching a conclusion first and then interviewing people for supporting quotes—and start becoming nothing more than satellite outposts of the RNC and DNC beamed directly into American living rooms and station wagons 24/7, that's when this country is in trouble. There's a difference between being a media professional who holds certain beliefs and core values and being a partisan hack.

That's what this book is about: the need for independent media that is free from the influences of the powerful—corporate and political. Only media that is connected to, and funded by, the people can legitimately inform and serve the people.

The authors are especially qualified to write on this subject, having been both on the receiving end—as most Americans are— of crappy mainstream media news, but also as the founders of an independent media alternative, *Citizen Radio*.

A few years after Rupert Murdoch launched his mission to destroy our civilization, a stoned, failing comic and a confused "writer" who had never been published met at a bookstore in New York City. Retail at a *bookstore* in New York attracts strange types. It's sort of like being at a party full of expats. See, most people working retail in Manhattan are aspiring somethings: actors, playwrights, singers. So by working retail, we were inherently failing at our professional goals, but since we were failing *at a bookstore*, we were also *pretentious* about it. "Oh, you need to know where the register is? Did you know I've read *all* the *Harry Potter* books?" No one is actually working that job. They're all standing around shooting the shit on their way to something better, something worthy of their talents and student loan debt.

The authors were no exception. We were pathetic human beings. Jamie had worked at the store for about a year before Allison's first day. This was the longest he'd held a job. The second Allison walked into the store, he was ready to make a move. In New York City, there's no time to waste. It's like when you're a nerd in high school and a new kid moves into town. You have a very short window to ingratiate yourself before they start to figure out no one likes you and they should steer clear.

Allison had made plans to join the Peace Corps after graduating from college in Illinois, mostly because she had been an English major and upon graduation realized her $108,000 degree was worthless. But in the interim, she'd decided to throw herself on the mercy of the minimum wage, which is when she'd stumbled into the bookstore and immediately recognized her tribe of fellow slackers. She decided to forgo traveling for the exciting life of retail work.

Well . . . she'd "decided" . . . and the Peace Corps interview hadn't gone so great.

Interviewer: So why do you want to join the Peace Corps?

Allison: Uhhh . . . I just graduated and I'm not really sure what to do with my life now.

Interviewer: . . . Would you say you're feeling lost?

Allison: Yeah! That's a good word for it!

Interviewer: Maybe like you're panicking a bit and looking for an escape?

Allison: . . .

Interviewer: . . .

Nailed it.

So on Allison's first day on the job, all Jamie saw was a new female employee entering his line of vision. Excitement! But not just *any* female. A female in a Superman shirt! This was it, he thought. This was fate. You see, Jamie also owned a Superman shirt—a Superman shirt he usually hides from women.

The plan was very simple. Allison was being trained by one of the managers, who was such a nice guy you could get away with murder right in front of him and his response would be to whisper, "Please make that the last time." So Jamie decided he would walk up, ignore the poor bastard, state to the new woman that he too owned a Superman shirt, spin around on his heels, and walk away like it ain't no thang.

Side note: The moment when you meet the person you're going to be with for the rest of your life is a difficult thing to describe. It's not a moment of lust. It's not like when you see someone in a bar that you want to sleep with and think: *Wow. That person is fucking hot.* It's not like that. When you meet your soul mate, it's more like: *Oh, shit.*

About halfway toward Allison, Jamie had his *Oh, shit* moment. Suddenly, he was doubting his entire plan. *Superman?! For fuck's sake, man.* But it was too late. He was already face-to-face with Allison and their tiny, wide-eyed manager. As the words "I have that shirt" were leaving his lips, he realized that he *didn't* have that shirt. Allison was wearing the very girly version of the Superman shirt he owned, so instead he muttered (at a very fast pace), "Ihavethat shirtnotagirl'sshirtIdon'thaveagirl'sshirtI'mnotagirl," and then speed-walked away.

The manager looked at Allison like a fatigued war veteran and said, "That's Jamie."

Maybe he was trying to play matchmaker, or maybe he was trying to get fired and free himself from his hellish retail bonds, but for some reason that same manager set it up so Jamie would train Allison.

Here's why that could be a fireable offense: Jamie had never been in charge of training *anyone*, mostly because he was known as the worst employee the store had ever seen. Unless he was in charge of training Allison to steal books, or hide under the information desk to avoid mean customers, there was no reason he should have been placed in charge of this task. But that's what happened.

They did zero work and talked about everything. Politics, books, Bill Hicks, things you typically hide from people you are trying to impress, all of it.

Jamie was so desperate to keep the conversation going that he asked if she wanted to go on break with him and said he would buy her coffee. That doesn't sound like a big deal, but at the time he had no money. Most people at the bookstore were full-time employees, but some of them still needed to rely on food stamps, money from their parents, and second jobs. Despite being broke, Jamie was determined to buy Allison coffee because he knew he had to keep talking to her, or resign himself to a lifetime of reading comic books and sadly masturbating.

They walked to a nearby cafe, ordered coffee, and when it came time to pay, Jamie confidently took out his wallet like the gentleman he was, accidentally opened it upside-down, and not only did *no money* fall out, but instead a sole, crumpled packet of Splenda he'd stolen from another cafe because he couldn't afford sugar slowly floated to the ground like an autumn leaf.

Together, they stared at the packet like they were looking at a dead body. Allison, quickly sensing Jamie's rising terror, grabbed her wallet and paid. Take THAT, gender norms! It's been love ever since.

This all happened in the summer of 2005, right after George W. Bush won reelection and millions of progressives' hearts were crying tiny emo tears. Additionally, Fox News was still at the height of power, but the failure of mainstream media to accurately report the news remained on the back burners for Allison and Jamie because they were *artists*, starving artists, who weren't actually doing any art because working retail is hard, draining stuff, and when they got back to their apartment at night, they just wanted to smoke weed and watch *Family Guy*. Because they'd *earned* it.

But that all changed one day when Jamie, desperate for a monumental shift in his life, dragged Allison behind the business books section (of all places) and proposed a radical idea: they quit their jobs, they drive around the country where Jamie would do small comedy gigs for money, Allison would write from the road, and they'd make a living that way—as true bohemians.

Dimly, Allison recalled her Peace Corps interviewer's voice: "Panicking a bit and looking for an escape?"

"Okay," she replied.

That summer, the internet exploded with alternative media: independent outlets—free from corporate masters—that could act as a check on America's seemingly endless occupations of Middle Eastern countries, institutional corruption, and mainstream media more interested in pleasing their advertisers than in reporting hard-hitting news. There were bloggers and shows like *Democracy Now* doing really exciting, intrepid journalism—not parroting party memos, but reporting facts and interviewing people who aren't CEOs and old white senators.

And the only way journalists can get those stories and hear those voices is if they step away from the computer and speak with people. You can see where we're going with this.

Living and working on the road is an amazing experience because you actually get to meet the people Washington is screwing over and not just see them in quick-cut TV montages set to Sarah McLachlan songs that make you cry at two a.m. when all you want to do is watch reruns of *30 Rock*. WE ADOPTED TWO CATS, OKAY, SARAH?!

It's easy to feel smug and secure in your political beliefs when all of your friends who work at the bookstore with you agree with everything you say. You pretty much get to drink venti lattes and act smarter than the "dumb hillbillies" (a.k.a. the vast majority of the country that doesn't live in New York City or L.A.) with zero consequences, since you live in your liberal hub with your liberal friends, and your liberal cats and your matching Superman shirts.

That smug security is tested when you drive through the South and meet the gay kid who can't come out of the closet out of fear for his safety, or the poor black family who is still struggling to recover from Hurricane Katrina, or the kid whose parents made him join the military because that's what people in his town do and he can't imagine a different future even though he's terrified of being sent to war. People have major problems in our beloved liberal city hubs, too, but a lot of us moved there to escape suburbia or the rural South, and like a scene out of the *Walking Dead*, journeyed to New York City where we found our people—our tribe.

Being on the road for a year radicalized the authors beyond our comfy liberal bias, and that was a direct result of these stories— the ones you can't find on basic cable. On cable news (with a few exceptions), if there's a panel to discuss immigration, that panel is composed of rich white dudes, and the occasional lady. A panel on the poor? Rich white dudes. An hour on racism in America? White dudes and rich Michael Steele. A panel on women's rights? They literally make the women leave the building. It's no wonder most people in this country are politically apathetic. No one is speaking for them. Who wants to watch CNN when David Brooks is on to talk about the plight of the Latina housekeeper? David Brooks, that's who.

One freezing winter evening in Ohio, Allison and Jamie were staying with a local hip-hop group, who apparently count Dennis Kucinich as a fan (naturally). The lead singer put on a news show called *Democracy Now*, and we were instantly paralyzed. A lady host?!?! What is this, the *lesbian* channel?!?!

It was a NEWS SHOW that actually showed NEWS STO-RIES. And get this madness: there were MINORITIES on the show: a real-life Latino—and wait, not just as a guest, but as a COHOST. And the actual host was a LADY! It was chaos. A progressive news show that didn't even need to show a liberal bias to get on the air. It just showed the news, and let the facts speak for themselves. It had guests we had never heard of: women, people of color, poor people, radical intellectuals, Noam Fucking Chomsky.

Our minds were blown. This was our own personal unicorn: "independent media." *Democracy Now* didn't have CEOs of banks come on to tell viewers how great their banks were, but instead interviewed the families whose houses those banks foreclosed on. The only way you would have seen a story on Honey Boo Boo is if she was leading a workers' strike in South America.

It's a little difficult to take cable news seriously when in between every segment on people dying from lack of affordable health care, millions losing their homes during the recession, and workers dying in horrific sweatshop conditions overseas, they play commercials for companies that profit from overpriced health care insurance, offer crummy mortgages, and supply us with cheap clothing made of orphan tears, plus the occasional Google or Nike ads, which are TOTALLY EVIL, but are made by Don Draper geniuses that know how to make Jamie cry. Emotionally manipulative bastards.

It's hard for a news show to give an unbiased report on health insurance companies dropping sick people from their coverage when those companies are paying for ad space on the network that airs the show. *Democracy Now* was not beholden to such companies, but because of this their audience was smaller, their budget more demure. Your mom and dad aren't going to stumble upon shows like this because *Democracy Now* doesn't have a Super Bowl–sized commercial budget.

As important as shows like *Democracy Now* are, they weren't (and still aren't) getting the kind of mainstream attention they deserve, although that particular show is very well known and very loved within left-wing circles.

But anyway, back in Ohio, on our hip-hop friend's couch, the authors decided we wanted to do a show like *Democracy Now*—a show that would speak on behalf of real people and real issues—but we also wanted to be funny about it. Jamie had learned about politics through comedians like Bill Hicks and George Carlin, and he decided humor could be a good educational tool for people who felt disenfranchised from the political system and burnt by a mainstream media that led the country to war based on a lie, or for people who lacked a formal education and felt intimidated by the often complex, opaque world of politics. Allison, who was formally educated, wanted to use humor as well, mostly so people wouldn't hear an hour of horribly depressing news and want to kill themselves. Allison has always been the more practical one.

After two years on the road, which we won't get into here,* we made it! And by "made it," we mean, "barely had enough to scrape by and got a one-room—not one bedroom, but one room total, like, for everything—apartment in a stabby area of Queens." There, we decided to start *Citizen Radio*.

When our parents asked what our plan was, we said, "We're making a radio show," and when they asked what channel it's on, we responded, ". . . Well, it's not ON the radio, per se, it's a

---

*Note to the editor: it's a riveting tale of two young souls pursuing their dreams while overcoming the odds! Second book, perhaps?

podcast on the internet!" And when they said, "The place with all the porn?" we said, ". . . Yes."

And when they *still* seemed unsure about their children's life decisions, Jamie realized he'd omitted a key detail of The Plan.

"Oh, THAT'S why you're so freaked out!" Jamie said. "Don't worry, Mom and Dad, we're going to be famous!"

Sighs, all around.

From its first days, *Citizen Radio* redefined the term "low-budget." Using a free online service, the authors would call in to an online soundboard via cell phones and record the show. We wrote headlines, did weird bits, were self-deprecating, and somehow found a new tribe—our listeners—once again. People seemed excited at the idea of learning along with us, instead of being talked down to or yelled at by partisan blowhards on the news.

The show started to take off, and for a while the authors thought maybe we could go mainstream. Maybe because we were young and told jokes we could get ourselves onto a big network and disguise our left-of-left agenda.

Well, *Citizen Radio* had two chances to go mainstream and they both ended in flaming wreckage. We won't use real names, but one opportunity came from a "music" channel that doesn't play any music, and the other was, um . . . CNN.

Usually, when going in for meetings like the one at the non-music music channel, the first people you meet are the young idealists. They're the ones that purposefully put *The Nation* magazine on the coffee table when you arrive, are legitimately liberal, and aren't old enough to have all their dreams crushed yet. So obviously they thought our ideas were SUPER! And we were like, "We did it!"

Then you have to meet with the VPs. Now, the VPs don't want you to think they are square, so before they shoot you down, they want to show you how cool they are. One VP we met with kept desperately trying to insert the fact that he was Canadian into everything he said.

"Now, look, of course *I* agree with you that the war is bad. I mean, I'm from CANADA!"

It was very weird, guys.

Eventually though, there came a time during pitching when someone inevitably mentioned that we'd need to play to middle America.

"Now, I'm not some dumb Midwestern idiot. I mean, guys, I'm FROM CANADA where we do cool Canadian things, but what about loser Iowans who aren't from the birthplace of Bret 'The Hitman' Hart?!"

Apparently, in Canada, you think you are better than all other people even while pandering to your boss and being too chicken-shit to take a stand. ANYWAY. They then cut to the chase:

"Will you be having Republicans on to balance the show?"

"No."

"Why not?"

"Because if you want to see Republicans, you can turn to every other fucking show on television."

"But you have to show the other side."

"Sometimes, there isn't another side. With gay rights, there is not another side. It's the right side versus the bigot. During the civil rights movement, you wouldn't say, 'Here is Martin Luther King, Jr., and from the other side . . . the Klan!'"

They laughed, then said good-bye. We said, "We did it!" Then we never heard from them again.

The second meeting, with CNN, was even crazier. For this one, the authors skipped meeting with the young ideologues and went right to the horrible boss people. Both of them (a lady and a gent) were characters right out of *Entourage*, which they totally watch but NOT ironically.

The guy spent the first fifteen minutes trying to show us the view—not the show *The View* because that would have been amazing—but the view from the actual room we were seated in.

"Look at that! That's what you will get if you work here!"

And then he repeated it over and over again, like he personally built the park we were looking at. But he hadn't built it. CNN hadn't built it. The one thing he had to boast about wasn't even their accomplishment. It was Central Park, for Christ's sake. Maybe it would have been impressive if he'd said, "Look at that ice sculpture!" and Anderson Cooper was down there, wearing goggles, using a high-powered chainsaw to create his frozen masterpiece.

When we finally stopped discussing the view—again, not the TV show—they asked what we wanted to name our show. Since we were very new at this and not creative we wanted the word "democracy" in the title, an homage to our heroes over at *Democracy Now*. Jamie gave a long, awesome speech about how making young people feel like they matter and have a voice would be our main goal—finally making them feel like they live in a participatory democracy.

Both of the execs took deep breaths, like someone had just punched them in the liver.

"Ohhh . . . democracy?" dudeman winced, looking at his lady counterpart.

"Um . . . yeah . . ." she winced back, worry mirrored in her eyes. "That's a little radical, don't you think?"

"Yeah . . . that's like, um . . . very 1940s."

And there you have it. That is a true story. One of the biggest news stations in America thought our system of governance was a little too radical and belonged in a traveling freak show, a.k.a. back on an internet podcast very far away from Central Park. CNN got one thing right: America is a little 1940s right now with the economic recession and tens of millions of people having lost their homes—not that they connected those dots, since they haven't bothered to seriously cover Wall Street corruption, the homelessness pandemic . . . and . . . anyway. You see why they gave Wall Street sweetheart Erin Burnett her own show. They really have their finger on the pulse of America!

The authors were sad, but not surprised. We weren't quite sure why we ever thought two podcast hosts could change cable news, but that was when we realized we didn't even want to change cable news. We wanted to change *the news*! Instead of having big donors or commercial sponsors that we had to pander to, we would have thousands of small donors, so we would be beholden to no corporate interests. And if you couldn't pay, you'd still get the shows for free, and if you could pay, you knew you were getting the backs of all the *Citizen Radio* Maniacs that couldn't afford to support the show more than by listening. It was, by far, the worst plan in the history of business! But it worked. And it worked because of the message.

Because of our listener support, we can say whatever we want. And we have. We were one of the first shows to start playing raw audio interviews from Zuccotti Park at the start of the Occupy Wall Street movement. We started commissioning young radical journalists to do field pieces on our show, and they know they can say whatever they want because we have no sponsors we are afraid of losing. And we pay them what they deserve to be paid, which is not what many established, far wealthier, so-called lefty websites pay, i.e., nothing.

• • •

It never paid to be independent more than when Fox News's Glenn Beck went after our humble little podcast. You see, the authors don't like Glenn Beck and his fear-mongering, polemic style, so we made it our mission to drive the hyperbolic host insane. We did this by interviewing his number one and number two enemies: ACORN's Bertha Lewis and cofounder of the Weather Underground Bill Ayers . . . on the same day. Oh yeah, we also may have called the episode our "Fuck You, Glenn Beck" episode.

This was after the anti-ACORN hysteria was at its height and Congress voted to defund the group that had previously worked to register voters and find affordable housing for poor people. And yet Glenn Beck *still* obsessed over ACORN on his television show. Lewis came onto *Citizen Radio* and accused Beck of committing "political necrophilia." Beck's website, *The Blaze*, picked up on the story and Beck talked about the comment later on his show.

The Blaze may have also fixated on *Citizen Radio* because Bill Ayers started to do semiregular appearances on our podcast. Ayers first became national news when his few brief encounters with then–Senator Obama spiraled into controversy after Sarah Palin accused Obama of "palling around with terrorists."

Ayers appeared on *Citizen Radio* a few times for a segment the authors named "Pallin' Around with Bill." For Sarah.

The Blaze quickly picked up on the story.

"I googled '*Citizen Radio*' and they are giving this NUT JOB BILL AYERS a weekly segment on their show!!!" one *Blaze* commenter cried.

Soon, more of Beck's minions came after us, and by "minions," we mean, like, twenty to thirty old people who didn't really know how to use Twitter. Usually there was an avatar of the American flag or a bald eagle, followed by an angry and confused tweet that said something like, "GO BACK TO RUSSIA HOW DO I HANG THIS UP? MARTHA!"

But a few of the minions tried to find sponsors to write to, to tell them to stop supporting us. Well, the joke was on them! No sponsor would ever give us money! HAHAHAHA. Some of the Becksters were so desperate, they started emailing our tattoo artist, thinking he was somehow an official sponsor of our show instead of simply our friend who occasionally tattoos us in exchange for a mention in the thank-you section of our website. He joyously forwarded the emails on to us.

In six years of being involved with independent media—watching shows like *Moyers & Company* and *Democracy Now*, and meeting and interviewing people like Jeremy Scahill, Naomi Klein, Matt Taibbi, Cornel West, Amy Goodman, Bertha Lewis, and so many more, we've learned a lot about journalism.

This is the most essential thing: You cannot be a news program and be afraid to cover the news and to stand up to bad people and bullies because of concerns over money. You cannot be afraid to criticize the White House or Wall Street because you want to get invited to the Correspondents' Dinner.

The news must be entirely independent from business and politics, otherwise we're left with the empty carcass of our establishment media in which "journalists" kiss up to the wealthy and powerful to remain in their Rolodexes, so they can keep the wealthy and powerful as anonymous sources the next time the wealthy and powerful want more tax breaks or to lead us into another pointless war.

The good news is, as the authors moved into a slightly larger apartment and eventually got married, and the United States invaded multiple Muslim countries with the near-total complacency of the establishment media, which was busy doing other things like *totally ignoring* the massive issues of climate change and our vanishing civil liberties, alternative media was on the rise. People were tired of the news getting the story wrong and they were looking elsewhere for the truth. That's how a little underground political podcast called *Citizen Radio* found its audience and started to grow.

Eight years, over a thousand podcast episodes, and countless documented protests later, the authors feel qualified to report on the rise of alternative media, the need for independent journalists and committed activists, and to shine a light on the massive failures of mainstream media along the way.

This book will highlight some of the media's biggest #newsfail—from underreporting the biggest story of our time, climate change—to leading the country into occupations of multiple Muslim countries, to providing crappy coverage of monumental cultural moments like the Occupy Wall Street movement, to failing to inform the public about the wasteful War on Drugs and the expanding police state, and how the left shouldn't hope for progressive messiahs like Jon Stewart to save them.

Listen up, this is going to be good.

CHAPTER 1

Jon Stewart Shrugged: How a Comedy Program Became the Most Trusted Name in "News"

The first comic Jamie ever saw live before deciding to dedicate his life to stand-up comedy was Jon Stewart at Carnegie Hall. Actually, that's not true. His *first* stand-up show was *The Amazing Johnathan* at the Stress Factory. But which sounds more romantic? Honestly? Political satirist at the most prestigious venue in Manhattan, or the yelling prop magician in New Brunswick, New Jersey?

He still remembers the show fondly. Watching Jon pace the stage with a tiny microphone talking politics while saying the F-word in a place designed for the most beautiful music in the world. There was still hope.

See, there was a time in America when Jon Stewart, the host of *The Daily Show*, was for many Americans the most trusted name in news. Not the most trusted name in comedy, but *news*.

That time has passed.

More than fifteen years after its debut on a network whose name should have given us a clue to the show's true allegiance, *The Daily Show with Jon Stewart* (which premiered in 1999 after giving Craig Kilborn the old heave-ho as the original *Daily Show* host) has gone from an invaluable bullshit detector on a government waging unjust wars on a mad hunt for nonexistent weapons of mass destruction, to, at best, an armchair activist's watercooler conversation starter ("Hey, did you hear what Jon Stewart said last night?" "Yeah, I feel like I know everything there is to know about the Middle East now. Want to hit up the falafel cart for lunch?") and at worst, a "news" program that's as guilty of cheerleading some of President Obama's worst offenses as Fox "News" was of rooting for Dubya's never-ending wars.

For eight years (1999–2007), *The Daily Show* served as a platform for the underdog: the marginalized, the voiceless, the stunned citizens watching their country march off to invade a country that never attacked the United States. Sure, America didn't have a Walter Cronkite for the twenty-first century, but at least they had a comedy show that could occasionally fill in for the role of decent journalism. With Jon Stewart at the helm, *The Daily Show* skewered the government and President Bush with vicious satire at a time when no establishment media outlet was making a serious effort to hold the powerful and elite accountable.

The Daily Show has always been at its best when it performs the role of archivist—that is, comparing what a politician says today with what he or she said last month. That's technically what a good journalist is supposed to do—call powerful people out when they lie or pander by saying, "No, no, but see . . . this is what you used to believe. Why the change?"

Through the early 2000s, *The Daily Show* and its host were truly counterculture. So it makes sense that during the Bush administration, which featured #newsfail ranging from the infamous

WMDs that never existed to the original fuckup that gave us Dubya (the Florida recount) to the establishment media framing massive tax cuts for the rich as a way to "create jobs," liberals turned Jon Stewart into their messiah. Unfortunately, that trust was misguided. No single news program, network, or individual— let alone a man who has consistently attempted to point out that he is a comedian, not a journalist or newsman or revolutionary— should be burdened with leading a cultural revolution.

That was never Jon Stewart's role. And he knew it. America just didn't want to listen, and we had nowhere else to turn.

As discussed, the authors were early adopters of Jon Stewart (the comedian, not the "journalist"). Jamie had always been obsessed with stand-up and Jon Stewart's HBO special was the one that he and his mom would watch on every holiday, every sick day, every time they had an excuse. There was a Middle East joke, a smart-bomb joke, religious jokes, and a joke about New York City apartment locks that Jamie can still quote on command.

He took stand-up super seriously. This was back in the day where if you wanted to record something off the TV so you could listen to it over and over again, you had to be crafty. We didn't have robots back in the dark ages, or flying DVDs, or whatever you kids use today. Jamie didn't even have a VCR. He had a boom box that he would place next to the speaker of the TV, which was turned up to full volume, and then he'd walk the perimeter of his house like a tiny fascist librarian to make sure everyone was quiet since the boom box would pick up any and all noises.

Hence, most of his mixtapes sounded like this:

Comedian: So what's the deal with white people trying to dance?!

Laughter.

Door slams.

Mom: Jamie, I'm home!!

Comedian: I mean, have you SEEN them try to dance?!?!

Jamie: Shut up, Mom! I'm recording!

More laughter.

Mom: Oh, I'm sorry! Maybe you didn't want the food I bought you!

Comedian: Their dance looks a little something like this . . .

Jamie: I DO!! BUT SHUT UP I'M RECORDING!!!

Mom: DON'T TELL YOUR MOTHER TO SHUT UP!!!!!

Sound of comic dancing and crowd clapping.

Jamie: Sorry, Mom.

They were truly the most pathetic mixtapes in all the land, but he had *tons* of them—filled with every bad comedy special from *The A-List*, to *An Evening at the Improv*, to *Lounge Lizards*. No one knew what a huge comedy nerd he really was until he met Allison. He was so jaded and used to people having terrible taste in comedy that he didn't bring up the subject to many of his friends.

In other words, Jamie was a hipster before hipster was cool, which is *the most hipster thing ever said*.

But we digress.

When Allison and Jamie met, he was surprised that the first thing Allison asked him behind the bookstore information desk was, "So you do stand-up?"

Jamie responded like a hipster moron and said something like, "Not the kind of stand-up you would like," and what Allison should have done was beat him to death with the info desk's big red telephone.

But instead she said, "Well, what kind do you do?"

"Not like Carrot Top," Jamie responded vaguely, possibly sneering at her, he can't remember, and again, what Allison *should* have done was taken the pen sitting next to them and stabbed him through the heart, then picked up the big red telephone and started smashing the back of his head like he was a zombie who had come to eat her young. Instead, when she heard him say "Carrot Top," she said:

"Ew, gross," and pretended to vomit.

They were soul mates.

Jamie and Allison immediately agreed on a handful of comedy truths: Bill Hicks is God, Carrot Top sucks, and Jon Stewart was the fucking *man*. That was 2005.

The Cure for Crappy Media Is Not More Crappy Media

You might wonder how, over the next eight years, a comedy show became the most trusted name in news. Well, if you turned on Fox News in 2008 you might have heard that Barack Obama was a Muslim, then an hour later that he's a Nazi, then at eight o'clock, *BREAKING: America Has Its First MUSLIM-NAZI President.*

The next morning, the weather guy might have whispered, just before commercial break, that they were misinformed about the "Muslim-Nazi" thing, but we should all still keep our eyes peeled, just to be safe. This kind of thing is par for the course on a network created by a lunatic Australian trying to become the king of media.

Of the major networks, CNN and MSNBC are slightly better, only because they at least try to hide their bullshit by occasionally inviting a person of color on their panels, and aren't so cartoonish about peddling their propaganda. However, these networks all still court the same advertisers, and largely the same agenda where war is a force for peace, capitalism is king, and the poor are invisible.

Fox News just has more ads for gold, which makes some sense, we admit, since poor people can't afford gold.

It's highly problematic, for example, when America's lovable doctor Sanjay Gupta goes on CNN and says inaccurate things about Michael Moore's *Sicko*. Gupta accused Moore of fudging the facts when critiquing the US health care system. Gupta's big "gotcha" moment was when he pointed out the World Health Organization ranks Cuba's health care system lower than the United States, a fact the filmmaker actually shows in his film.[1]

Gupta then accused Moore of reporting inaccurately that the American health care system spends $7,000 per person on health, whereas Cuba spends $25 per person. Gupta said this is untrue and the United States actually spends $6,096 a year per person versus $229 a year in Cuba.

But according to the Department of Health & Human Services, Moore's figures are closer to correct than Gupta's. US per capita health care spending was projected to reach $7,092 in 2006, and $7,498 in 2007, the year *Sicko* was released.

Additionally, Moore said Cuba spent $251 per person, not $25, as Gupta claimed.

Gupta tried to argue the projected numbers were somehow invalid, but in the same discussion, cited another projection— Medicare's looming insolvency—as a reason not to support expanding the program.

The good doctor then went on to accuse *Sicko* of being misleading about the different kinds of health care afforded to citizens.

The film is filled with content Canadians and Brits sitting in waiting rooms, confident care will come. In Canada, you can be waiting for a long time. A survey of six industrialized nations found that only Canada was worse than the United States when it came to waiting for a doctor's appointment for a medical problem.

But as Fairness & Accuracy in Reporting (FAIR) points out, this is a grossly misleading characterization of the Commonwealth Fund's comparative study of first-world health care systems. Instead of stressing that the study found that the United States did better than one country with universal care in terms of waiting time, Gupta could have instead focused on the fact that four out of five of the universal health care countries studied, including Britain, outperformed the United States.[2]

The study Gupta cited actually placed the United States as the *worst overall of all the health care systems studied*, placing it last or next to last in all but one of eight criteria, while the United States spends almost twice as much per capita as the next more expensive system.

This was truly cherry-picking journalism at its worst, but people watching think: *Well, he's a doctor, for God's sake! Why wouldn't he want me healthy?! Sanjay wouldn't lie! He loves me! Michael Moore is the partisan! This is the most trusted name in news!* But by the time the retraction comes, it's too late.

Just ask the Iraqis.

NBC's *Meet the Press* let Dick Cheney on air to reference a story given to the *New York Times* by an anonymous figure within the administration, and the former vice president used that platform to lead us to war.[3] That's like a prank an especially evil Zack Morris would pull on Mr. Belding, not something that should happen on one of the most "respected" news shows in the world!

Then there is the liberals' beloved MSNBC.

Turn on MSNBC, that socialist bastion of lesbian propaganda, and you see Chuck Todd talking about the importance of bipartisanship, sandwiched in between his trusty segment about—seriously—the White House soup of the day (I HOPE IT'S SPLIT PEAS!), Michael Steele being taken seriously for some reason, three to thirty-five hours of Joe Scarborough, Chris Matthews gushing over George W. Bush's package in a flight suit, and more.

Hurray! Liberals!

Look, it's okay for a station to have voices like that, balanced by Rachel Maddow, Melissa Harris-Perry, and Chris Hayes, but (and here's where a thing called "false equivalency" comes in) not when you are known as the left-wing version of Fox News.

False equivalency is when someone falsely equates an act or idea of one thing as being equally egregious to that of another thing when that comparison isn't actually fair or valid.

See, viewers naturally assume, based on false equivalency, that if Fox News is as right-wing as it gets, MSNBC is as left-wing as it gets, and consequently that their programming is as extreme as that of Fox News (which it is not, hence a "false" equivalency).

Oftentimes, MSNBC actually peddles the mainstream Democratic Party platforms, thereby alienating many leftists who are dissatisfied with Democratic leadership. They think: *Gee, if I don't have a home on the so-called left-of-left MSNBC, where **do** I belong?*

This is where *The Daily Show* came in.

It was a false liberal ascription that befell Jon Stewart's "newsroom" and turned it from a comedy show on a corporate television station that was very funny and provided an entertaining reprieve from life's suckage into a show that routinely expressed outright contempt for *actual* counterculture activities and yet has also been called "the most trusted name in news." (See, we promised we'd tell you how it happened.)

Less cartoonishly strident than Fox, but more critical of the left than MSNBC, this equal-opportunity comedy show takes potshots at all comers and therefore . . . they must be the actual news!

Turns out, that is not only inaccurate, but just as dangerous as giving the fire-breathing terror-mongers over at Fox News the title of "fair and balanced."

("I'm a comedian first," Stewart once said in an interview with Fox News's Chris Wallace. "My comedy is informed by an ideological background, there's no question about that. But . . . I'm not an activist. I am a comedian."[4])

For many young liberals, new to the political system and in many cases just coming into their right to vote, *The Daily Show* began to fill their outrage quota of the day, right after your roommate eating the last of the Corn Pops and leaving empty beer cans in the sink. It's fun and easy to watch a TV show and then feel no need to take further action.

Why protest the war?! Jon took care of that on Tuesday!

That's not Jon's fault. But the Rally to Restore Sanity was.

The Rally to Restore Sanity: Caring Is Uncool and Superlame

On August 28, 2010, Glenn Beck, still at that time a ratings rain-maker in the Fox News empire, held a "Restoring Honor" rally on the steps of the Lincoln Memorial where Martin Luther King, Jr., once delivered his "I Have a Dream" speech. The original purpose of this rally was to promote Beck's new book *The Plan*, but then he decreed that the rally "would not be political," but rather would be a "celebration of America's heroes and heritage."[5]

Many civil rights leaders of the black community criticized Beck for picking the anniversary of King's speech to hold the rally. Rev. Carlton W. Veazy, minister in the National Baptist Convention and former president of the Religious Coalition for Reproductive Choice, accused Beck of "hijacking" King's legacy.

So obviously that rally was really weird and crazy, and Jon Stewart and Stephen Colbert mocked it for being weird and crazy (Stewart dubbed it the "I Have a Scheme" rally, which we still find amusing), then decided to have their own party. At first this seemed like really great news. Sometimes it takes a comedy show, or a music scene, to rally young people, and word was that tens of thousands of kids from all over the country were flying in just to participate in the event.

But soon it became clear that the Rally to Restore Sanity and/or Fear—Fear being Colbert's contribution—was entirely an exercise in satire and not at all an exercise in activism. In fact, it appeared to have been solely created to draw a false equivalency between grassroots efforts on the left to combat corporate greed and corruption and the Dick Armey–funded Astroturf campaign called the Tea Party.

The following message was posted on *The Daily Show*'s official Rally to Restore Sanity's Facebook invite:

"I'm mad as hell, and I'm not going to take it anymore!"
Who among us has not wanted to open their window and shout that at the top of their lungs?

Seriously, who?

Because we're looking for those people. We're looking for the people who think shouting is annoying, counterproductive, and terrible for your throat; who feel that the loudest voices shouldn't be the only ones that get heard; and who believe that the only time it's appropriate to draw a Hitler mustache on someone is when that person is actually Hitler. Or Charlie Chaplin in certain roles.[6]

Under the motto "Take it down a notch for America," and in the spirit of similar orations like JFK's famous "Meh" speech, hundreds of thousands of individuals converged on Washington, DC, protesters carried signs pleading for "sanity" in political discourse, and many aimed that critique at Glenn Beck-esque figures who frequently engage in rhetorical hyperbole by derailing conversations while screaming "NAZI!!" at their political opponents.

Unfortunately, since that false equivalency between the left and right was drawn from the genesis of the rally, the Stewart/Colbert critique also seemed to say that any passion for reform whatsoever, no matter how grounded in reality, is uncalled for. That it's never okay to shout, even if that shouting has something to do with holding people accountable for murdering innocent Iraqi children. Also, it's uncool.

And if it's just a happy fun-time variety hour on "Comedy" Central, that's one thing. The authors, as dedicated activists and lovers of comedy, understand Stewart's comedic prerogative even if we don't always agree with it. But, despite his protestations to the contrary, Stewart has to know that a late-night show watched by millions of Americans per week, and constantly lauded as "the most trusted name in news" maybe, just maybe, has some responsibility not to make a total mockery of the democratic process when given a platform for encouraging real grassroots involvement on the scale that his rally attracted.

Or does he?

Rachel Maddow asked Stewart about the rally's false equivalency during an interview on MSNBC:[7]

On the issue of the perception of the rally in media . . . Bill Maher's criticism of it was this. He said, "When Jon announced his rally, he said that the national conversation is dominated by people on the right who believe Obama is a socialist and people on the left who believe 9/11 was an inside job. But I can't name any Democrat leaders who think 9/11 was an inside job."

Stewart responded:

The intention is to say that we've all bought into—the conflict in this country is left and right, liberal/conservative, red/blue. All the news networks have been [sic] bought into that. . . . And what it does is it amplifies a division that I actually don't think is the right fight. . . . But what I do believe is: both sides have their way of shutting down debate. And the news networks have allowed these two sides to become the fight in the country. I think the fight in the country is corruption versus not corruption, extremists versus regular. Do you understand what I'm saying?

Hmmm. No, we don't. Is Jon Stewart saying choices are hard? That taking a stand is lame?

That "division" he dismisses is literally the only fight that matters—it's between the people who think corporations should be allowed to bleed the country dry, and those fighting for Wall Street reform. It's between those who don't believe in waging war based on a lie and those who seek military hegemony over the Middle East. The "division" is the whole reason we have political choice—or the illusion of it. We're supposed to fight in a democracy! We're supposed to be loud and boisterous and occasionally hurt each other's feelings.

Otherwise, what you have is a bunch of milquetoast puppets agreeing with the supreme leader all the time, a.k.a. a dictatorship. Stewart appears to be aware of this fact, alluding to a fight between "corruption" and "not corruption," but apparently he wants that fight to take place someplace far away, preferably in quiet voices, and God forbid anyone carries any aggressively worded signs.

Again, it's not Jon Stewart's fault that our media has labeled his show this way. But when story after story comes out saying college students get their news from *The Daily Show*, and at the same time, over at Fox News and in the mainstream discourse we hear about just how left-wing *The Daily Show* is, it sets a dangerous precedent. If I'm someone who is new to politics, and I hear the allegedly radical-left Stewart & Co. start to bash activists, I'm going to think, *Well, if even* The Daily Show *is making fun of them, maybe they are going too far.*

When they made the journey to Washington, *The Daily Show* disciples were clearly searching for something. Maybe it was community, maybe it was a road trip just to get out of their hometown for a few days. But what they got was a lesson in apathy with a sound track from (why, God, why?) Kid Rock.

Rock performed his song "Care," which could serve as a manifesto for the disempowered:

> *I can't stop the war*
> *shelter homeless, feed the poor. . . .*
> *I can't change the world and make things fair.*
> *The least that I can do is care.*

What the hell does that even mean? On second thought, it's pretty self-explanatory. Yes, Kid, the very least you can do is care.

Jon Stewart and Comedy Central brought 200,000 kids together, many who made their first journey to Washington, attended their first political event, who maybe even for the first time met people of the same political leaning, who met other gay kids, other artists, other students drowning in debt, and they got Kid Fucking Rock to sing about NOT doing anything?!

This might be where *The Daily Show with Jon Stewart* officially abdicated its Most Trusted title, spending all of its hard-earned capital on what could have been a truly inspiring, energizing event honoring participants in the great American institution of democracy but instead became one bloated, crass exercise in satire-for-ratings. We guess this is how some people felt about Seth MacFarlane hosting the Oscars.

The Rally to Restore Sanity and/or Fear was like if Martin Luther King graced those stairs and said, "I had a dream, but it's not really important to talk about right now. Just know that bad things are happening to black people, but I guess bad things always happen, so never mind. We can't change anything. Hey, at least we aren't slaves anymore! Am I right?! NO CHANTING!"

The Daily Show Exposes History's Greatest Monsters: Wall Street Protesters

In September 2011, the world felt like it divided into two versions of reality. There was the reality on the ground at Zuccotti Park and then the "reality" presented in the mainstream media.

Allison spent a lot of time in the Occupy Wall Street camp, interviewing students who were buried under tens of thousands of dollars in student debt, workers toiling away in three different jobs (and still finding time to protest), and people who had struggled to find a job in the hostile economic environment.

But then she went home and turned on the news. According to many news outlets, the Occupy movement did not comprise an overwhelming majority of peaceful, ordinary citizens who were tired of the country's class divide and Wall Street's unscrupulous practices. Rather, according to sources like CNN and Fox News, Occupiers were dirty, smelly hippies who were too lazy to find real work.

The Daily Show was quick to jump on the hippie-punching train.

The show ran a hit piece on Occupy in October 2011 in which correspondent John Oliver wandered around Zuccotti Park, encountering some of the protest's stranger characters.

"How amongst the 99 percent did I still feel like I didn't fit in?" too-cool-for-collective-action John Oliver wondered aloud, before consulting with "the 98 percent of Americans who might agree with the protesters' message if it weren't for the protesters themselves."[8]

Because, you know, The Daily Show loves Occupy! Just not the Occupy composed of the Occupiers, who are bad and silly and smelly.

In November, just a couple days after Occupy Wall Street was evicted from Zuccotti Park, *The Daily Show* aired another hit piece with correspondent Samantha Bee interviewing the most stereotypically spacey Occupiers she could find sleeping at the camp. That's not to say there aren't those elements within Occupy, but it was alarming to see *The Daily Show* fall into the same habits of hippie-punching seen in the establishment media.

The Daily Show's message to its audience was clear: Occupy Wall Street is weird. Don't join them.

Again, in Stewart's defense, he is not the only writer on *The Daily Show*, and he clearly never wanted to be assigned this role of progressive leader.

He really couldn't be more overt about it. So no one should have been surprised when Stewart, whose brother, Larry, worked as the chief operating officer of NYSE Euronext (2010–2013), the parent company of the New York Stock Exchange, didn't really seem to *get* what Occupy Wall Street was pissed off about.

Many liberals were shocked—shocked!—that *The Daily Show* completely ignored the one-year anniversary of Occupy Wall Street, one of the most important grassroots movements to ever occur in the United States. But they really, really shouldn't have been.

Occupiers are just, like, so *totally* uncool to still be on this whole "Wall Street" corruption thing.

According to Stewart and *The Daily Show*, activists who "glitter bomb" homophobic politicians are acting like "petulant children,"[9] and Occupy Wall Street is a bunch of scatterbrained hippies who don't truly represent the 99 percent. This is hardly a show that has its fingers on the pulse of the activist community. If the authors were given to copyright infringement, they might publish the following as an appendix in this book:

The Daily Show's Guide to Activism

1. Wake up.
2. Play Xbox for one to seven hours.
3. Throw away empty PBR cans.
4. Write angry Tumblr post about evils of corporations while smoking Marlboro reds, eating McDonald's hamburger, and drinking Pepsi beverage.
5. Watch *The Daily Show with Jon Stewart*.
6. Email MoveOn.org petition to family.
7. Avoid phone calls from family members.
8. Change Twitter avatar to whatever color for whatever latest third-world country is being destroyed by crazed dictator.
9. Search Wikipedia for information on said country in case later quizzed.
10. Play Xbox for several more hours.
11. Go to sleep with self-satisfied smile on face.

Real activism doesn't work that way. You can't appoint a progressive messiah and listen to him snipe through your flat screen and expect for things to magically get better.

The only way to effect real change is through the precise instances of direct action that *The Daily Show*—supposed bastion of liberalism—repeatedly mocks, not only in brief comedy sketches on late-night TV, but on a grand scale such as the Rally to Restore Sanity.

In conclusion: Never trust a show owned by Viacom to lead a counterculture revolution. If *The Daily Show* was ever a real threat to the establishment, it would have been canceled years ago.

CHAPTER 2

Get Your Flaming Arrows Ready: Class War and the Media That Mocks Protesters Fighting It

When Keith Olbermann is the first major journalist to cover your rally, you know you're in trouble. But the media's Occupy Wall Street reporting extended even beyond their usual problem of undercoverage.

Many mainstream pundits and journalists actually seemed *angry* at the movement. They seemed less concerned with what Occupy stood for (fighting institutional corruption and class war), and more concerned with mocking activists from within their corporate media towers.

Few journalists took the time to go to Zuccotti Park or the other occupations across the country to speak with protesters, preferring instead to pontificate about the futility of protest from their comfortable Aeron office chairs. This is a problem because there is no way to get an accurate sense of the consequences of class war unless you are on the ground in the midst of it. It's like calling yourself a war correspondent because you occasionally watch MSNBC and have strong feelings about Richard Engel's fabulous hair.

The authors got to experience this lesson firsthand when Allison drove Jamie to the hospital in Baton Rouge, Louisiana, after he punched through two panes of glass to rescue a monkey named Wobbles.

Let's back up for a minute.

In the brief interim between quitting the bookstore and hitting the road, we were doing what all fancy artists do—living with Jamie's mom. It was Jamie's birthday, but not much could cheer him up because he was in his twenties, living with his mom, and he and his then-girlfriend/future wife had to sleep in his youngest brother's old bed that was so small Jamie would fall out and crash onto the floor at least twice every night.

Much like the 38 million Americans living below the official poverty line in 2005, we didn't have any money, so Jamie wasn't expecting a gift for his birthday, but when he woke up, fell out of bed again, and brushed his teeth, he walked into the living room and found Allison waiting on the couch, holding a tiny gift bag, which Jamie would soon discover contained a pint-sized stuffed monkey. Allison picked up the monkey, walked him along Jamie's arm up to his shoulder, and made the little guy punch Jamie in the face. She said, "That's Wobbles!" and we both started to laugh. Hard. In fact, it was the most we'd laughed since we failed at life and had to move in with Jamie's mom.

And so the myth of Wobbles was born.

While we drove across the country, Wobbles sat on the car dashboard, "danced" to terrible nineties music, and kept us entertained on ten-hour stretches of driving through the flat Midwest or the mountains of Montana. Half-delirious during these times of extreme poverty and overcaffeinating, we created a backstory for him: Wobbles was an Amazonian Punching Monkey, a failed businessman, a Republican henchman, and an alcoholic racist, who every time he was called out on his shit, would pretend he was two years old and act cute so nobody could be mad at him. He may or may not have also worked for the Nixon administration, although he would deny it.

Wobbles became the mascot of our journey, the mast to our pirate ship. We took him *everywhere*. Eventually, after we stopped sucking at life and got our acts together, we took pictures of Wobbles in London phone booths and even in Beijing's Tiananmen Square (the monkey SWEARS he had nothing to do with "the incident" that took place there).

Most significantly, Wobbles was the force behind an event that truly enlightened us to class war in America.

Jamie got booked to do a show in Baton Rouge, Louisiana, and the host of the show was kind enough to let us crash on his floor afterward. The plan was to do the show, sleep over, and in the morning we'd drive nine hours to Oklahoma for another gig. Since the host had to work the next day, he told us to close the door behind us after we left and it would lock automatically.

Everything went according to plan, but the next morning upon crossing the bridge to leave the city, Jamie asked Allison where Wobbles was. Allison asked Jamie the same question, and the authors realized that for the first time ever *we forgot him*.

Jamie spun the car around and bravely started to cry, and Allison tried to keep us both calm. We called our host, who oddly enough could not leave his important job to let us back into his home to retrieve our stuffed monkey, and we didn't have the time to wait or we would miss the fifty-dollar gig that awaited us in Oklahoma. But there was no fucking way we were leaving Wobbles.

No monkey left behind!

We showed up at the house and started pacing outside, trying to figure out how to break into our lovely host's home. The house itself was exactly what you picture when you think of the South: old, wooden, ivy growing up a trellis on the side, and creaky steps that led up to the back porch and door.

Allison ran around front to investigate and try to find a way inside while Jamie climbed the steps and looked around the back. He peered through the window into the guest bedroom and saw Wobbles. That motherfucker was just lying there. Mocking us. Just like Nixon would have. When Jamie pushed on the first pane of glass, it moved a little. He pushed in and up, which is when his hands smashed through not one but two sheets of glass. Glass from a very, very old window that looked like it was riddled with hepatitis. His arms were covered up to his biceps in shattered glass, and so he did what any man would do.

He screamed, "Allllllissssssssooonn!!!!"

Allison ran to see what the hell was going on. When she arrived, Jamie had taken his shirt off and wrapped it around his finger to try and stymie the geyser of blood located where his pinky used to be. He had little cuts everywhere, but his left pinky was where the pain was coming from, which made sense because it was hanging on by only a few tendons. He started to go pale as he asked Allison repeatedly what he should do.

We didn't have money for an ambulance, we had no idea where we were, and Allison was hoping Jamie was exaggerating about the pain.

He wasn't.

Jamie revealed his finger, which was hanging off at an unnatural angle, and Allison, wide-eyed, stared in horror at his hand before she shouted:

"OH MY GOD IT LOOKS LIKE YOUR FUCKING FINGER IS GOING TO FALL OFF!!!!"

Panic. We ran to the neighbors' homes, Jamie shirtless and covered in blood, as he pounded on the doors and hoped someone would answer.

Understandably, no one did.

The authors then decided to jump in the car, and there is a good chance one of them shouted, "Wobbles, we will be back for you!"

We sped off.

Important detail: Allison did not have a valid driver's license, but she didn't hesitate as she tore through the streets of Louisiana, one hand on the wheel, the other fumbling to dial 911 on her cell phone. Allison explained—well, shouted frantically, to be accurate—their situation to the operator, who agreed to relay directions to the emergency room to Allison, and then in the thickest southern accent imaginable cried, "Sugar, I'm gonna get you to this hospital!"

Phone cradled against her shoulder, Allison weaved in and out of traffic like she was fleeing from the cops, while their southern angel asked for landmarks so she could guide them to the emergency room. Weirdly, Allison unconsciously started to mimic the operator's accent in the heat of the moment. Jamie thought he might be hallucinating when she shouted, "Got it, girl! Making a left on Georgia Ave! Oh, lord!"

We got to the hospital and immediately walked into chaos, since the community of Baton Rouge—like many poor places in Louisiana—was still (and still is) reeling from Hurricane Katrina. The emergency room was packed on a Tuesday morning, and everybody in line had been waiting for hours. We were the only white people there, and the only ones that weren't used to this kind of treatment (oh, white privilege, you so crazy). Jamie used to work security at an emergency room in Princeton, New Jersey, the whitest place in the entire world, where if an old rich person came in because they were sad and weren't seen within fifteen minutes, they threw their cocktail at the nearest minimum-wage worker.

Finally, after seven hours, Jamie was taken into another room where nurses propped him up on a bed and told him to wait. Eventually, a doctor showed up and poked around in his open wound, checking to see if the pinky would need to be amputated or not.

"Well, it all depends on if this last ligament is severed," he said casually. Jamie gripped Allison's arm with his good hand.

"Is it severed?" Jamie asked, in excruciating pain and trying not to stare at all the blood lest he faint.

"Hmm . . . let me get a second opinion."

Then the doctor left and they went back to waiting. Jamie looked at Allison and asked, "Did he just go get a friend to see if they need to cut off my finger?"

Jamie spent the waiting period coming to terms with maybe losing a finger, which involved coming up with jokes about having nine fingers that he could use to open his act.

Eventually, a second doctor appeared, prodded around Jamie's finger a little more, and declared he believed they could save the pinky.

And they did! Kind of. They stitched Jamie up, but there was extensive nerve damage and he still can't really bend it, but the point is he still has five fingers on that hand. One may not work, but whatever!

After leaving the hospital $3,000 poorer (which was all of our money in the whole world that we needed to save for things like car repairs, food, and shelter), the authors returned to our host's home. Even though Allison and Jamie had destroyed his property, he refused to let them pay for the damage (as if they had any money to do so), and even cooked them dinner. Toward the end of the meal, he said, "So what did you guys need so bad that you had to break into my house?"

Of course, Jamie lied and said, "Oh . . . my notebook. You know how it is. Can't leave your art behind."

The host looked at them and said, "Okay, man. Hey . . . by the way . . . it didn't have to do with that little monkey by the bed, did it?"

Jamie and Allison both acted surprised: "What? A monkey? Oh, that little thing? Yeah, we can take that, too."

The point of this story is: all journalists are sort of like disaster tourists. They visit an affected area like post-Katrina Louisiana, get a taste of what life is like there, and then leave to write up their thoughts from the comfort of their own home—usually a big, safe city somewhere in the first world.

The authors were kind of like that on the road. Our brief, memorable, extremely bloody experience in a Baton Rouge emergency room couldn't ever truly enlighten us about what it's like to live permanently in an impoverished community hit by an unimaginable force of nature and then be abandoned by the federal government. However, even that small taste of class war did permanently change our perspective on how America has become a two-tiered society of haves and have-nots where some people (rich, often white individuals) possess access to life's amenities, and poor people of color are being left behind.

The Wobbles Incident took place before the Affordable Care

Act clusterfuck—when President Obama was privately meeting with huge insurance companies and Republicans were accusing the president of being a socialist for not wanting people to die because they lacked coverage.

But remembering the Baton Rouge emergency room incident while surrounded by individuals in tremendous pain made that story personal, and that's when Allison figured out an important part of covering a story is stepping away from the computer and actually speaking with people in the affected zone, whether it's a genocide in Rwanda, or an emergency room in a state with soaring health care costs and understaffed hospitals still recovering from a storm that cost taxpayers an estimated $125 billion, or a group of anti–Wall Street activists being villainized and dismissed by the mainstream media. The job of a journalist is to amplify the voices of the marginalized. To do that, you have to hear those voices in the first place.

Upon returning from the road, feeling wiser but wearier, Allison decided she wanted to be a journalist (instead of an illegal ambulance driver), but she quickly discovered this was easier said than done. Many of the outlets whose thresholds Allison could reasonably expect to cross as a new journalist (and even later as a not-so-new journalist) expected her to work for free or close to free. Her first "gig" was at Huffington Post—quotes included because the job didn't pay. For HuffPo, she wrote occasional philosophical blog posts about these damn kids who don't care about protesting these days, that usually ended up sandwiched between posts from Ben Affleck plugging his latest movie, and *Wings*'s Steven Weber shaking his fist at those darn Republicans.

She also freelanced for a magazine about exotic travel desti-
nations and products for rich people, which was a somewhat de-
moralizing experience considering she was paid pennies per word
working from the authors' studio apartment in Queens. Furthermore, her editor frequently tried to stiff her on pay, so she regularly
engaged in hour-long screaming matches with him over the phone,
whenever she could reach him in his Trinidadian bunker (FOR
REAL).

Eventually, she got slightly better jobs at slightly better blogs
that at least paid a bit more than her articles about the "Five Best
Yachts for Your Global Voyage." But freelancing remained a strange
journey. For example, one day in 2010 she wrote a takedown of
Kelsey Grammer's new project, *RightNetwork*, a television channel
devoted to all things right-wing (because apparently we needed
another one). A week later, Allison received a package in the mail
from, you guessed it, *RightNetwork*. Upon opening it, she discovered a moldy pie.

What the hell? Was this some kind of mob message? *Mess with
Grammer and you get the moldy pie.* As vegans, we were doubly
concerned about a horse's head coming next.

Allison tweeted something to the effect of: "@RightNetwork:
Why the hell did you send me a moldy pie??"

They quickly responded that it wasn't meant to be moldy—that
it was a tongue-in-cheek thank-you for giving the network some
publicity, but it must have gone bad in the mail.

A couple days later, Kelsey Grammer himself recorded a personal thank-you to Allison and posted it on YouTube. Of course,
there was no way he could know that, unlike most people, Allison
didn't know him from his hit television show *Frasier*. She knew
him from his voice-over work on *The Simpsons* when he played

Sideshow Bob, a villainous murderer hell-bent on killing Bart Simpson.

So when Kelsey Grammer appeared on the screen and purred: "Allison Kilkenny . . ." in that sinister voice, Allison responded:

"AHHH!! SIDESHOW BOB!!!" and nearly threw her laptop out the window.

RIP *RightNetwork* (2010–2011). It was a weird, very short ride.

Allison segued from hit pieces to beat reporting around the time UK Uncut, an anti-corporate anti-tax-dodging protest movement emerged. A US version sprung up called, appropriately, US Uncut, and Allison began writing about it for *The Nation*. The group was made up of a small group of solid organizers, but the protests never really got off the ground.

However, soon after she began covering US Uncut, many of the organizers joined another burgeoning movement: Occupy Wall Street.

On September 17, 2011, a small group gathered in New York City to address concerns such as being buried under crushing student debt, getting kicked out of foreclosed homes, and the overwhelming corruption of Wall Street. According to certain mainstream news outlets, this gathering signified that *Batman* villain Bane's horde of murdering murderers had invaded lower Manhattan. And worse, they needed jobs!

Actually, at first, Occupy wasn't anything to write home about. Around a hundred protesters gathered near Wall Street—*near*—not even *on* Wall Street. At the time, Allison wrote in *The Nation* that the protest certainly didn't live up to standards set by activists in Tahrir Square and Spain. To be quite frank, it seemed like a flop. Then, one of the activists walked up to Allison, who was standing with a group of other independent journalists (the only kind following the activism beat at the time) and said, "Don't leave yet. We're moving to another location."

"Where?" Allison asked.

"Zuccotti."

And still, when protesters made the move and started setting up tents in Zuccotti Park, the general sense was the occupation would be broken up in a matter of hours.

But it wasn't, and though many initially dismissed the movement entirely, there were also some early believers.

Media to Occupy Wall Street: Y U Mad, Bro?

Contrary to popular belief, OWS was not a Phish parking lot party disguised as a protest. No one asked if visitors wanted to buy "dank weed" or trade a ticket for a grilled cheese. In fact, not only was it attracting protesters of every gender, race, sexual orientation, age, and occupation, but well-known academics were making regular visits, speaking publicly, and even teaching, from Nobel Prize–winner Joseph Stiglitz, to Cornel West, Naomi Klein, and more.

OWS quickly transformed from just a protest movement to a cultural event.

At one point, one of Occupy's younger (and we assume more misguided) organizers emailed Jamie and asked if he wanted to perform some of his trademark rants—like he did that one time on Conan O'Brien's show that resulted in him never being invited back on (more on that later). Jamie wasn't interested in using Occupy Wall Street to boost his career (and let's face it, associating with OWS at that time wasn't exactly a resume-builder), but *Citizen Radio* wanted to help the cause, so Jamie, in true professional form, responded with something like, "I don't know if anyone gives a fuck about me, but if I can find someone way more famous to go on after me, I'll do it."

Oddly enough, every big-name comedian he reached out to who claimed to be on the left either said no, or didn't reply to Jamie, which was a bit disappointing to say the least. These were people getting paid handsomely to go on TV and complain about "the man" and now they had a chance to actually do something, and thought it was too risky or just didn't care enough to help out.

Luckily, about a month before receiving the invitation, Jamie had half-joked on Twitter that he wanted to get a Noam Chomsky lower-back tattoo ("half-joked" means he was deadly serious until Allison threatened him with divorce, hence changing it to a half-joke). Somehow, hip-hop legend Talib Kweli saw this tweet and thought it was funny enough to start following Jamie on Twitter. Talib was last on the list of people Jamie wrote to about the OWS invite. Comedians will do anything for attention, and usually spend their afternoons feeling sorry for themselves with no additional capacity to feel sorry for others, but *musicians*? Musicians are cool. They spend their afternoons rolling around in gold coins, Scrooge McDuck–style. The thought of bringing someone as iconic as Talib down to OWS made the authors nervous to even contemplate. This is the guy about whom Jay Z rapped: "If skills sold, truth be told / I'd probably be, lyrically, Talib Kweli."

Talib wrote back right away because musicians have soul and comedians have dead clowns for hearts. He was game. The only thing he asked was if he could be shown around the camp before performing. WHAT A DIVA!

The authors and some OWS organizers walked around with Talib as he tried to keep a low profile. Talib was very humble and seemed genuinely curious to learn how the camp at Zuccotti functioned.

Then, Jamie and Talib stood on a wall and performed for the occupiers. The crowd was silent and when something needed to be said louder, protesters invoked the "People's Mic"—a strategy used by activists to naturally amplify their voices in which a group repeats a line of dialogue from a single person in order to make the statement louder. (The use of bullhorns is prohibited in many cities without a permit.)

Jamie went first and performed two rants. Often, when the OWS crowd liked what a speaker was saying, they would silently wave their fingers in the air (this gesture, meant to express appreciation without drowning out the performer, is called spirit fingers). Jamie loved watching them do this during his set, but the lack of applause did provoke the comic in him to think, *Um . . . the people watching the live stream are going to think I'm bombing.*

Good thing he wasn't doing it for his career!

But forget spirit fingers—when he introduced Talib, the park was electric. It wasn't just about music, or a celebrity sighting in lower Manhattan. This moment was just one more piece of validation for a burgeoning movement, one more story for the history books. Talib's Zuccotti intro can be heard on the first track of his album *Prisoner of Conscious*, and opens with "Mic check . . . Mic check . . . I am at a loss for words . . ." which was how most supporters felt at one time or another watching the struggle grow.

And it grew quickly. No one had ever seen anything like it, and the corporate media's initial, defensive response was to villainize the movement. CNN's Erin Burnett smeared the protesters as being philosophically inconsistent because they demanded Wall Street reform, while simultaneously owning iPhones;[1] and the *New York Times*'s Andrew Ross Sorkin ominously penned that the group didn't seem brutal ". . . at least not yet."[2] All the while, the mainstream media obsessed over elements like the drum circle at Zuccotti Park, as though the movement was nothing more than a gathering of bongo enthusiasts.

The coverage was borderline schizophrenic. *Occupy Wall Street is a gang of thugs! Who also smoke weed and accomplish nothing!*

When portraying Occupy Wall Street as a band of hell-raising single mothers didn't stick, the media instead went for the "dirty hippie" angle. *Did we say they had guns? We meant dreadlocks.* As opposed to being the Threat to End All Other Threats, occupiers suddenly became a bunch of stargazing kids who just don't get how the real world works. They're spacey. They're too disorganized ideologically. They need to *get a job.* And no, touring with Phish is not a job.

Seriously, you have no idea how many wealthy tourists and Wall Street traders yelled "Get a job!" at the Occupy protesters, as though that wasn't *exactly* one of the key reasons hundreds of protesters set up a camp in Zuccotti Park. *They couldn't find jobs,* geniuses. Or, they did have a job—sometimes more than one job—but those jobs didn't pay very well (thanks, capitalism!), and they were still buried in debt.

That's like screaming at antiwar protesters: "Hey! Why don't *you* try to end the war?!"

The fact is, there was such a wide range of people at Zuccotti, you could never put them into a single category. We interviewed a nurse who had recently been laid off and would take his children to school, then stand in solidarity with the protesters in between job interviews. People would come down on their lunch breaks, before or after work, or between classes. Our favorite sign of the movement sums up many of the occupiers' lives nicely: "Lost a job, found an occupation."

The critique most leveled at OWS, *too scattered ideologically*, is absurd given there is a *lot* wrong with the country right now, and if one carefully thinks about the various Occupy slogans, it's actually quite easy to see how demanding fair wages is tied to reforming capitalism, which is tied to student debt, which is related to the prison reform movement, and ending the War on Drugs, and fighting for taxpayer-funded elections, which is in turn tied to the housing market. Lots of the "little people" are getting squashed by this rabid behemoth named capitalism, and that exploitation has many different facets, but the root cause is always inequality. No one was saying during the civil rights movement: "They want to ride in the front of the bus ANNNND drink from the same water fountain?! Are they from different *planets*??"

And yes, being scattered ideologically eventually became an impediment to progress, but in the initial first phase of Occupy, it was simplistic for media to shut out the movement as being "unserious" because OWS was claiming *too many things* are wrong with the country. If anything, Occupy presented a highly disciplined, scaled-back version of their grievances, and at other times, managed to encapsulate the disillusionment of an entire generation with its six-word slogan: *Shit Is Fucked Up and Bullshit*.

Speaking of Fucked Up and Bullshit: The Media

In the *New York Times*, columnist Ginia Bellafante wrote a confused critique of the OWS movement in week one of its existence.

She first claimed a Joni Mitchell look-alike named Zuni Tikka, whom Bellafante describes as "half-naked" and "dancing on the north side of Zuccotti Park" was a "default ambassador" of the movement, and then, in one of the following paragraphs, described the protest as "leaderless."[3]

And things went downhill from there.

The more serious, newsworthy aspects of the early days of Occupy—such as the penning and macing of innocent protesters at Union Square, for example—were completely ignored by Bellafante, who chose instead to wonder why kids these days don't get off their couches and put down their Xboxes to take to the streets and demand class equality.

"It is a curious fact of life in New York that even as the disparities between rich and poor grow deeper, the kind of large-scale civil agitation that Mayor Michael R. Bloomberg recently suggested might happen here hasn't taken shape," Bellafante wrote.

Instead of proposing an explanation for why that "large-scale" agitation had not yet materialized, she first dismissed the effort entirely, and then wondered—in the New York Times, mind you—why these little fledgling movements can't seem to get off the ground. At one point, Bellafante nearly fell ass-backward into an explanation when she described a young man who stopped by Zuccotti only in "fits and spurts" because his mother feared he'd be tear-gassed by the police. It sounded as though Bellafante was on the cusp of critiquing the US police state that has completely terrified the activist community into near-submission, but then . . . not so much.

The job of the journalist is to find and speak for the voices that don't have enough amplification to be heard: the powerless. The dudes with the pepper spray and guns? They have power. The

White House has power. Wall Street is going to be fine. They have plenty of ways and plenty of cash to get their message out, but the senior citizen who was just hauled off by the police for demanding better health insurance, and the students who were maced for the violent act of "sitting," they're the ones who need journalists to tell their stories.

Look, it's easy to find crazy people at any protest. In large groups of people, it's a statistical inevitability that at least a few individuals are going to have some very worrying thoughts about the spacemen living in their teeth, but taking those disturbed individuals and presenting them as any kind of status quo is intellectually dishonest, not to mention shitty journalism of the lowest caliber.

Sure, there are Zuni Tikkas in Occupy, but so what? Personally, we'd rather hang with Zuni, who appears to be guilty only of dancing in the drum circle and not wearing a suit to, say, Wall Street criminals responsible for millions of Americans losing their homes.

Furthermore, the Zuni Tikkas were by far the minority within Occupy, and it would have been super easy for Bellafante to figure that out, had she bothered to sample a diverse array of protesters on more than a single day at the park to give an accurate depiction of the movement.

She could have spoken to Matthew Prowless, an unassuming forty-year-old father of two in a baseball cap, who attended the Occupy Wall Street protest, and stood with his friend by a group of black bloc protesters whom Matthew was eyeing curiously, like they were exotic fish in an aquarium. To his mind, the more eccentric aspects of the protest ("protest yoga," for example) were just distractions from the far more serious cause.

"My home has been seized, I'm unemployed, there's no job prospects on the horizon. I have two children and I don't see a future for them. This is the only way I see to effect change. This isn't a progressive issue. This is an American issue. We're here to take our country back from the corporations," he said, adding that he fears for the future of the United States where corporations can now spend unlimited, anonymous dollars to elect the candidates of their choice.[4]

BORING! Right, *New York Times*? More stories about rich teenagers and their fancy parties, please!

Matthew, like many Occupy activists and supporters, couldn't permanently occupy the park because he had to go home and care for his two children. The movement has always been bigger than the physical occupation of Zuccotti, but many journalists, like Bellafante, can't get past the drum circles.

Perhaps Bellafante and her peers were quick to dismiss OWS because one of the ways to gain status as a "serious journalist" is to treat protesters with contempt, and as unserious and useless idealists. To express interest or sympathy with activists means risking being labeled as an activist journalist—the worst insult among Beltway elites. It leaves a journalist vulnerable to being entirely dismissed by the upper echelons of Washington and their journo peers, which means no access to that beat. The safest path to take is the one in which activists are sneered at and belittled. It's a good way to get cozy with government elites, and maintain them as sources.

Then there was Andrew Ross Sorkin. Dear God, Andrew Ross Sorkin. Here's another reporter for the *New York Times*, who on the one-year anniversary of Occupy in which a large, peaceful turnout quickly devolved into police violently arresting more than 180 people, said the event had "fizzled."[5] That diagnosis was preordained considering Sorkin is the reporter who only first checked out what those Occupy hooligans were up to because he got a phone call from the "chief executive of a major bank" wanting to know how worried he and his CEO buddies should be about the movement. Sorkin dutifully hurried down to Zuccotti to check it out.[6]

Holding truth to power, like the best of them!

But when he did eventually make it down to the camp he was NOT IMPRESSED IN THE SLIGHTEST, you guys.

"They didn't seem like a brutal group—at least not yet," Sorkin wrote. Maybe he said that because they were currently getting the shit kicked out of them by the NYPD. It's difficult to be brutal when your face is jammed against a curb.

To his credit, despite the fact that he was only there in his capacity as a Wall Street lackey, Sorkin was able to discern a coherent message from the protesters: "The demonstrators are seeking accountability for Wall Street and corporate America for the financial crisis and the growing economic inequality gap."

Boom. See? Not that complicated.

But don't tell CNN's Erin Burnett that. CNN, being as "hip to the times" as Larry King at a rave, decided that, during a recession and after a massive Wall Street bailout, the people needed a fresh, new voice and so they hired Burnett—a current member of the Council on Foreign Relations and former Goldman Sachs analyst, who is married to a current Citigroup executive—and advertised her as "straight from Wall Street!"

Way to still have your finger on the pulse of America, you crazy CNN execs.

And this is the network that said *Citizen Radio's* ideal of democracy was "too radical." Ahem.

Viewers could practically see the vein on Burnett's head pulsate as she fought to understand why average folks would gather to protest against her beloved Wall Street. She crafted a segment called "Seriously?!" in which she made the claim that because protesters purchase products, they can't possibly simultaneously protest the unethical behavior of Wall Street.

In other words, if you have an iPhone, you can't also be concerned about worker-abuse practices in China's Foxconn factory. So, one probably also can't be worried about water quality control issues if one drinks tap water, or care about air pollutants if one is an air-breather. Mad at Nike? I hope you don't have feet!

Burnett commented that she "saw dancing, bongo drums, even a clown" at the protest, but its participants "did not know what they want," except that "it seems like people want a messiah leader, just like they did when they anointed Barack Obama."[7] Hey, you know what, Erin? At least that bongo-playing clown didn't steal our wallets, then when *he* hit the limits on *our* credit cards, call us to ask for a bailout.

Here is what we've learned from our on-the-ground, independent investigation into the Occupy Wall Street movement:

Occupy was a leaderless movement precisely because it did not *want* a "messiah leader." The group was a pure democratic force that literally voted on every decision, no matter how tiny, in the early days. For example, the general assembly voted on every single line in their declaration of demands and principles of solidarity to remain as inclusive as possible, citing all sexual orientations, gender identities, races, ages, and causes ranging from the environment to animal cruelty, to student debt, housing, and labor.

Occupy was NOT the Democratic Party, and despite the Democratic National Committee's consistent efforts to appropriate the language of Occupy (the 99 percent versus the 1 percent), the movement never became a branch of the party itself. In fact, if more members of the mainstream media had bothered to talk to the protesters instead of employing reductive journalism to produce sound bites for prime time, they would have discovered that Occupy activists were pissed off at President Obama, too, and were by no means "in the bag" for the Democratic Party. Instead, the most frequent complaint made at Zuccotti was that *both* parties are controlled by corporations, and don't represent the interests of the majority of Americans.

Sounds like a pretty interesting story for, say, a news establishment to cover. A democracy within a broken democracy. It's very telling that the corporate media spent a lot of time covering and inflating the numbers of the Tea Party gatherings, but were quick to dismiss OWS as being an unserious movement. One movement beseeched officials to be more extremist in their pursuit of rightwing policies, and the other challenged the very foundation of American capitalism. It's no surprise OWS lost that fight.

Despite the uninformed establishment-media coverage and near-constant police brutality, OWS protesters held their camp for almost two months, and by sheer force of will, steered the national dialogue away from an obsession over deficits to a conversation about class inequality.

It was in part due to Occupy's influence that President Obama called economic fairness "the defining issue of our time" during his State of the Union address in early 2012. Remember: this is America. Our presidents are trying to sell the American Mythology to everyone, the one about how anyone can achieve anything because George Washington and apple pie. So for a sitting president to talk openly about class is, in the words of one Joseph Biden, a big fucking deal.

Occupy changed how the establishment media partitions the

potential electorate as well. While the usual interest groups remain: the women, the gays, the blacks, et cetera, new classifications emerged: the 1 percent, the 99 percent, or in Mitt Romney's case, the 47 percent.

But without a capable, independent media, the class war continues to be an underreported story. When journalism is an exclusive club, the result is homogenized media that marginalizes voices, such as those talking in Zuccotti Park. That's why independent media is so essential. Alternative media must grow and become a viable option *that actually pays journalists* (looking at you, Huffington Post) in order to counterbalance the dominating corporate narrative peddled by mainstream media that kisses the ring of Wall Street and punches the underclass when they try to fight back.

CHAPTER 3

Al Gore Is Fat and We're All Going to Die: Or, You Can't Blame Climate Change on Vegans

In 2006, former vice president Al Gore debuted a film called *An Inconvenient Truth* that reflected a startling consensus among the world's scientists: *global warming is real.* It's man-made. And it's going to permanently alter the world unless we change our wicked human ways. Oh, and a ton of people will die unless we make those changes very soon.

Instead of pausing and considering the facts like adults, the right-wing media collectively lost its mind. Fox News immediately declared reality, and everything within reality—including global warming facts and figures—to be a big, giant hoax.

And also, they will have you know: Al Gore is fat. *Sure, Al. Where did you see these "facts"? On the INTERNET, which is ALSO not real?* Case closed, fatty.

Seriously, that's what our Very Serious Establishment Media decided to focus on as the world came to an end: the former vice president's weight. It's not like that's even a more tantalizing story. We would probably buy a paper with the headline: "MAYDAY!

MAYDAY! WE'RE ALL GOING TO DIE!" over "Middle-Aged Man Enjoys Food."

Yes, Gore packed on the pounds after leaving the White House—possibly because he read the hard data and saw that we're all going to die, and he chose to deal with this prospect by stress-eating.

But does it really matter if Al Gore is fat? Of course not. The real issue is that the earth is warming, our climate is changing, and that's why we're experiencing melting glaciers, stronger storms, droughts, and rising sea levels.

Many people in this country would rather burn to death than listen to someone with a different political affiliation speak the inconvenient truth. Even the most powerful media magnate in the world, Rupert Murdoch, has joined the climate change denial cult. The mogul took to Twitter to declare: "World growing greener with increased carbon," and "Thirty years of satellite evidence. Forests growing faster and thicker," and also, "Why not switch from useless renewable energy investment to real job-creating infrastructure projects? Many great possibilities waiting." The statements were a dramatic change for Murdoch, who six years earlier had declared, "Climate change poses clear, catastrophic threats."[1] As the *Independent* notes, News Corp's corporate position on climate change is very different from that of many of its news outlets, like Fox News and the *Wall Street Journal*. Perhaps Rupert was tweaking the message to suit his right-wing, climate-change-skeptic brands.

That's how bad it's become. Everyone's grandchildren are going to drown, burn, or be eaten by revenge-seeking polar bears, but Al Gore is a Democrat, and he knows Bill Clinton, so the partisan hacks make it about dumb partisan hackery.

And the mainstream media isn't doing much of anything to remedy this. But more on that in a minute.

First we want to say: Guess what, Republicans? WE DON'T LIKE AL GORE! We don't like Bill Clinton either! There! Now can we save the planet? Bill Clinton passed the Defense of Marriage Act, a piece of legislation so homophobic the Westboro Baptist Church has circle jerks while reading it aloud. All that deregulation that caused the economic crash? Also Clinton's work. And how about spreading the myth that music with explicit lyrics leads to violence? Stupid Al Gore and his stupid wife.

So there. Cards on the table. We hate Al Gore, too. Happy?

Now, back to what some of us (the authors are looking at ourselves here) might consider the GREATEST #NEWSFAIL OF ALL TIME.

Climate Change Deniers Declare War on Science

For some reason (okay, two reasons: ratings and ad dollars) the mainstream media—not merely the right-wing nutjobs like Glenn Beck—can't seem to give airtime to a politicized issue like global warming even though it might quite literally mean the extinction of our planet and the entire human race if people remain uninformed.

Every once in a while, a scientist sneaks past CNN's security and makes it on air, but even then the establishment media attempts to force "balance" in a situation where there IS NO OTHER SIDE. There are facts and numbers on the side of the scientists who say global warming is real and man-made, and then there are charlatans and Bible-thumpers on the other side, salivating over ExxonMobil's stock portfolio or gazing longingly at a photo of Jesus returning on his white stallion.

Here is every newscaster in the world hosting a Right vs. Left debate, on any issue:

Right Debater #1: X = Y
Left Debater #2: X = X
Moderator: I guess we'll never know!

NO! We DO know! Look up the facts, newsperson! You're on the news! You have like a THOUSAND computers behind you in that stupid newsroom right now! One of those computers must have Google, surely. Get your army of unpaid interns to find the answer!

It's not offensive for a newsperson to tell a guest that they're wrong. In fact, that's their job. What is offensive is not giving citizens the real news while calling *yourself* THE NEWS.

A 2011 Media Matters study found that nightly news coverage of climate change plummeted 72 percent between 2009 and 2011. Nightly news coverage on NBC, ABC, and CBS went from two hours in 2009 to just twenty-seven minutes in 2010 and thirty-eight minutes in 2011. Furthermore, the study found that the Sunday news shows consulted political and media figures on climate change, but left scientists (also known as "the only people with actual facts") out of the discussion. Of those hosted or interviewed on climate change, 50 percent were political figures—including elected officials, strategists, and advisers—and 45 percent were media figures, and *none were scientists*.[2]

In 2013, Media Matters also documented that Reuters's

coverage of climate change declined by nearly 50 percent under the regime of the current managing editor, Paul Ingrassia, who allegedly identified himself as a "climate change skeptic" (as reported by former Reuters climate change correspondent David Fogarty in 2012).[3]

It's a fact that, since 1991, roughly 97 percent of all published scientific papers that take a position on the question agree that humans are warming the planet, and yet, thanks to #newsfail, the real and necessary conversation has become muddled with propaganda.

Much of the confusion can be traced back to Fox News's relentless promotion of the fabricated "Climategate" scandal, which involved misrepresentations of emails sent to and from climate scientists at the University of East Anglia's Climate Research Unit.

In 2009, the server at the Climate Research Unit at UEA was hacked by an external attacker. Climate change deniers claimed emails between scientists showed that global warming is a scientific conspiracy, and alleged that scientists had manipulated climate data and attempted to suppress critics. *Telegraph* columnist James Delingpole popularized the term "Climategate" to describe the controversy.

From the beginning, the Climate Research Unit tried to explain that the emails had been taken out of context, but the media— mostly Fox News, Rush Limbaugh, and Glenn Beck—didn't want to listen because the out-of-context emails fit their political agenda. Fox News Washington managing editor Bill Sammon, famous for instructing Fox journalists to avoid using the term "public option" during the health care reform debate and to instead say "government option" in order to fool the public into siding against government (and their own best interests), also ordered his underlings to cast doubt on climate science amid Climategate.

Sammon sent out an email to the staffs of *Special Report*, *Fox News Sunday*, and FoxNews.com, as well as to other reporters, producers, and network executives, instructing them to "IMMEDIATELY" include objections of "critics" when reporting on climate data.[4]

Sammon wrote this email even though it was already clear by then that Climategate was a made-up scandal. Twenty-nine prominent scientists, including eleven members of the National Academy of Sciences, sent a letter to Congress stating that global warming is real, and the prestigious science journal *Nature* concluded "nothing in the e-mails undermines the scientific case that global warming is real—or that human activities are almost certainly the cause."

Independent reviews and Pennsylvania State University all found that the emails did not represent any scientific malpractice, yet the damage had been done. Fox News, and other networks and media outlets that gave the story traction, planted seeds of doubt in millions of Americans' minds.

This would be like if we at *Citizen Radio* had 100 million listeners all over the country and decided to fuck with them by broadcasting day in and day out that robots will soon enslave the human race, and refused to bring on any scientists that would provide any kind of rebuttal to our claim.

And in fact, we have done stories about climate change—including the effects of global warming on weather patterns, and how that change can result in catastrophic events like Superstorm Sandy. Whereas most media outlets are content to provide disaster porn, *Citizen Radio* and other independent media outlets are busy trying to explore why disasters happen in the first place, and how we as a society can prevent the next tragedy.

In summation: a 2013 CNN/ORC International poll shows a little less than half (49 percent) of Americans believe that climate change is proven and that it can be attributed to man-made causes.[5] Meanwhile, a shocking number of elected officials—55 percent of congressional Republicans in 2013—refuse to accept that climate change is real. *ThinkProgress* reports most states have at least one representative who denies climate change science, and it's even more pronounced in Republican leadership, where 90 percent deny climate science.

And wouldn't you know . . . the 157 members of the "climate denier caucus" have taken over $50 million in energy contributions over the course of their careers.[6]

When the media can't find consensus on something 97 percent of published scientific papers agree on, and the guests the media invite on their shows deny that climate change is real, it's probably safe to assume the media isn't planning to pick up on another very real environmental catastrophe that is even less popular than Al Gore at the semiannual Dick Cheney seal slaughter.

Eat Bambi, Destroy the World

It doesn't matter if you are at a 350.org, PETA-sponsored, Che Guevara–honoring, left-of-left meet-up in the "Anarchy Shack" built by the Howard Zinn organization dedicated to shutting down factory farms . . . if you ask the people around you if there is any vegan food available, they'll collectively declare, "Oh, JESUS CHRIST!"

Sure, the world is changing and a vegan lifestyle is becoming much more acceptable than it once was (mostly because we are all dying from eating shitty food), but there aren't many issues that still inspire such blind rage as when we tell someone we don't eat animals. If you thought this book was only going to reaffirm your brilliant beliefs in the failure of mainstream media, and now you fear that two preachy vegans are about to make you feel bad about dinner: take a deep breath, close the book, throw it against a wall, exhale, come back, and give it another shot!

We promise: we'll be gentle.

Allison has been a vegan for over a decade now, and when she first adopted this diet while living in the Midwest, food alternatives were fairly dire and included soy cheese that would evaporate in the microwave and a deluxe Subway "Hate Salad" package including lettuce, a whole "fuck you" tomato that they spitefully threw in, and an employee who'd punch you in the face at the register. Oh, and for a dollar extra you could drink your own tears. Jealous?

Jamie, on the other hand, waited about ten more years to go vegan—until he could get vegan pizza delivered, feast on vegan buffalo wings for "fight nights," make vegan lasagna, and pretty much eat like a (vegan) king.

Is Allison a better person than Jamie? Clearly, yes. Totally.

Jamie's path was, like everything he does, bumpy and full of screaming. He went from a stoned, fast-food-eating train wreck to a pretentious and unhealthy vegetarian, and now is the healthy vegan we know and love.

This is why he would never consider himself preachy. That would be like Pat Robertson lecturing people about tolerance. Plus, as with any group, there may be preachy members, but in no way is it the majority among vegans, most of whom are scared to admit in public that they don't eat "America's Meat," a.k.a. bacon. And vegans rarely go online taunting their carnivore friends with vegetable porn via Facebook or Instagram.

Hey guess what I'm eating right now? Mushrooms, you fucking girl!

Hey, @bassfisher, my cholesterol is TOTES amazing hows yours, NERD?!!

Waves tofu in front of meat-eating sister. Yeeeeah, you want soooome?!?!

That has never happened in cyberspace or on earth. Not once.

But back to Jamie. Did you know there is such a thing as a Pizza Hut/Taco Bell hybrid restaurant?! YUP! Now, this is important: not a Pizza Hut NEXT DOOR to a Taco Bell, but a Pizza Hut INSIDE a Taco Bell. That's the main reason Jamie can never be preachy about going vegan. He lived near one of these devil restaurants that delivered to his apartment, while he spent his days smoking copious amounts of pot and lusting after pizza-flavored tacos.

He remembers the first time ordering from the Pizza Bell (Taco Hut?). He got comically high and ordered both tacos and tiny pizzas, 'cause obvs. When the delivery guy got to the door, he only had one pizza box. Jamie got very sad, stupidly assuming that his dream of eating pizza with tacos was ruined. The driver, sensing Jamie's despair, put up one finger, as if to say, "Wait, my child." Then, he opened the pizza box in front of Jamie, and it was *lined wall-to-wall* with tacos and tiny pizzas.

It was the happiest moment of Jamie's life, promptly followed by the sickest he has ever been.

He had always wanted to be vegetarian *for the animals*, but unlike Allison, he lacked willpower, though when he was in high school, he did manage to remain vegetarian for two years. Problem was, he didn't like vegetables. So he lived off mac and cheese and pizza while assuming he was healthier than all of his much fitter friends. *Oh, you're eating chicken? You're gonna die. Time to make a pizza sandwich!* And then he would stack pizzas on top of each other and eat so much that every artery in his body let out a tiny scream followed by a really foul burp.

Eventually, a horrible mother of an ex-girlfriend snuck bacon into his soup, presumably so she could wag a finger in his face and say, "Ha ha! You're not so vegan now, are ya, boy!" and shut him up for good. As opposed to taking it on the chin, and starting his vegetarian life anew the next day, Jamie completely derailed and ate every meat product within sight.

Sorry, animals of 1998–2005.

When he was older and wiser, he met Allison and became vegetarian again. (Now he checks his soup!) In one of their first conversations, he proudly told her that he was a vegetarian, assuming that would make her weak in the knees. Such a sensitive man.

What are you eating for lunch, Allison? Seal Soup? Well, I'm an animal lover and better than you!

Allison smiled and said, "That's awesome, I'm vegan!" And Jamie maturely responded, "Aw, Jesus Christ." See, even vegetarians hate vegans.

Looking back, Jamie knows why he got so defensive. He was scared of change. He thought he would have to eat salad for every meal. Worse, he knew he would be confronted with facts. Terrible, terrible facts. Facts about milk and cheese and climate change.

See what we did there?

So Jamie's quest to become vegan began much like all good movements: not for the animals, or the earth, or the workers, or to feed the hungry, but to get the girl.

Meat was easy to give up again. You show most people a video of their dinner screaming as it's being skinned alive, and many of them decide to forgo eating animals. All Jamie needed was the added bonus of a cute girl to get back on the right path. However, it's harder to visualize how consuming dairy is cruel. You don't see the cows being raped (female cows lactate only when pregnant, so they're impregnated by things called "rape racks"), their udders so filled with chemicals that they are the size of small cars. You just see pizza. Glorious pizza.

Jamie had a tough time letting go of dairy. He wanted to be vegan, but would literally sneak out of the apartment after dark to go buy pizza on the corner. Like a drug addict.

It was so bad that if there is ever a *Behind the Music*–type special about Jamie, instead of the scene where the drummer ODs on heroin, it would be Jamie on the road, naked in a hotel bathtub, surrounded by stuffed-crust pizza boxes, sobbing to Allison on the phone: "YOU DON'T KNOW ME! YOU DON'T KNOW ME!"

But like any addiction, you find things to replace it. You educate yourself. You develop healthier cravings. And you stop being an asshole.

And guess what? There are vegans everywhere! They're in the NFL, UFC, and the Olympics (track star Carl Lewis is a vegan and he won ten Olympics medals, nine of which were gold!). You name the sport and there is a preachy vegan kicking its ass! It's hard to continue stereotyping vegans as the emaciated crybabies who, if you lightly bump into them, break all of their bones and turn into a pile of soy nuggets.

And veganism is no longer just the realm of the elitist New Yorker. Our favorite vegan burger is in Austin, Texas, and our favorite vegan Thai place is in Iowa. These are two states in which most people assume you will be hate-crimed to death if you tell anyone you're vegan. Well, no more! There's even a vegan strip club in Portland, Oregon!

Being a healthy vegan today is easy as long as you have reasonable access to fresh produce, and admittedly that luxury is not available to all Americans. Poor communities often have produce dry zones as a result of things like institutional racism, where grocery chains aren't incentivized to enter black and brown people's communities, and the US government subsidizing shitty food like corn. Well, corn isn't shitty exactly, but corn becomes this stuff called high-fructose corn syrup that is in all the foods you currently eat that are killing you. Because the government pays for high-fructose corn syrup, it's in a lot of food, and it's extremely cheap. Meanwhile, whole foods like apples and oranges are pricier because Uncle Sam isn't subsidizing them.

It's not impossible to be vegan with meager means—the authors managed to remain vegan while living out of their car, for example—but even though Allison and Jamie found vegan food in Iowa, Texas, the Netherlands, and even at Jamie's grandma's house, there are still big swaths of the country, particularly in poor urban and rural areas, known as "food deserts" where it's tougher to be a healthy vegan, or to eat healthy at all. This is why it's important for the government to stop subsidizing that shitty high-fructose corn syrup and start making fruits and veggies more affordable—but you're not going to see Matt Lauer start banging that drum on the *Today* show.

Now, some of you may be thinking: *Shut up.*

Fair enough. But we believe in you, reader. We believe you are a good person. So let's stop talking about what you eat. Instead let's talk about some other issues you may care about: labor, global warming, poverty, and animal cruelty.

If the Above Argument Didn't Tempt You, Might We Suggest Becoming Vegan to Prevent All of Our Fiery Deaths?

In 2010, the United Nations released a report that said a vegan diet was vital in saving the world from hunger, fuel poverty, and the worst effects of climate change. Now, we usually ignore everything the UN says since they're all a bunch of Muslim hippies, but let's take a look anyway:

As the global population surges toward a predicted 9.1 billion people by 2050, Western tastes for diets rich in meat and dairy products are unsustainable, says the report from United Nations Environment Programme's (UNEP) international panel of sustainable resource management.[7]

It further says the impacts from agriculture are expected to increase substantially due to population growth increasing the consumption of animal products. Unlike fossil fuels, it is difficult to look for alternatives: people have to eat. A substantial reduction of impacts would only be possible with a large-scale worldwide diet change, away from animal products.

In other words, the best way to be an effective environmentalist is to reduce or entirely eliminate your consumption of meat and dairy, but pointing this fact out to progressives tends to get them worked up, usually because they reeeeeeally don't want to give up bacon.

People's resistance to veganism is part laziness and part mis-education. Look at it this way: it's easy to support something like same sex marriage because, hey, if you're a guy and you don't want to marry other guys, no one is going to force you to do that in order to maintain your civil-rights street cred, but embracing something like veganism *does* require you to change your daily behavior.

Yes, there are those shifty hypocrites who claim to be deeply concerned about the consequences of factory farming on the environment and the corporate ravaging of the country as they shove McDonald's hamburgers down their throats, but there are others who harbor incorrect, preconceived notions of veganism that scare them away from changing their behaviors.

Why is that? We're glad you asked!

We live in a meat-dominated culture and it is easy to remain ignorant about what that means, because animal slaughter is not advertised on those packages of "all-beef" franks you suck down on the Fourth of July, and it's very rarely reported on in the main-stream press, whose six o'clock news hour is chock full of adver-tisements from Hormel, Oscar Mayer, and Perdue.

So those same nonexistent scientists who are not being invited on TV news shows to not talk about climate change, are also not popping up next to Diane Sawyer to tell you that, by whittling out the dairy and meat, you can help save the planet.

According to the Environmental Defense Fund, a nonprofit ad-vocacy group, if every American skipped one meal of chicken per week and substituted vegetarian foods instead, the carbon dioxide savings would be the same as taking more than half a million cars off US roads.[8]

The UN came out with a report in 2010 stating that factory farms are the greatest contributor to global warming.[9] Remember when crazy right-wing senator John Thune started laughing about hippies who think "cow farts" are destroying the earth? In 2008, Thune introduced a bill that would amend the Clean Air Act to outlaw the Environmental Protection Agency from regulating air pollutants that are known to contribute to global warming.

"There are things of greater cause of CO_2 emissions in our society, a lot of smoke stack industries, automobiles, but to think for a minute livestock production is contributing in a more significant way of global warming and greenhouse gas emissions than other sources I think is really almost laughable," Thune said.[10]

Except the joke is on Thune. Those cow farts produce methane, which, in large doses, is superbad for the environment. According to a 2006 report by the Food and Agriculture Organization of the United Nations (FAO), animal agriculture is responsible for 18 percent of all human-induced greenhouse gas emissions, including 37 percent of methane emissions and 65 percent of nitrous oxide emissions. In the United States, methane emissions from pig and dairy cow manure increased by 45 percent and 94 percent respectively between 1990 and 2009. Gross.[11]

Now, imagine what the effects would be if Americans cut out *all* meat and *all* dairy from their diet. Would some of those farmers have to find new jobs? Sure. But would you give up free health care for the good of the insurance salespeople? What about the people who make money off of subprime mortgages? Should we forgo banking regulations because it may disrupt their worlds? It would also be hard for farmers to make a living tilling crops as the earth burns.

This is another place government could play an important role: in crop and livestock transitioning. Subsidizing the transition from globe-wrecking crops and livestock would be a way to save the earth without unnecessarily destroying the livelihoods of hard-working farmers.

Besides, most of the meat you consume doesn't come from small-time farmers. People still harbor an image of Old McDonald at his little farmhouse, playing with his talking animals. The sad truth is that giant factory farms with terrible working conditions are more of a threat to these old-school farmers than the vegans who want to curb methane levels.

Think about how selfish it is to ignore these kinds of scientific studies.

Study person: Will you eat ONE veggie stir-fry a week to save the environment?

Joe USA: I don't know, bro. I reeeally like eating hamburgers . . . like . . . every day.

Study person: You're a dick.

Joe USA: Yes. Yes I am.

It's easy for liberals to see a Hummer driving down the street and feel smug as we emphatically flick off the driver, humor the idea of following him home, then slashing his tires, writing a threatening message on the door in human blood, and maybe breaking off the Hummer's antenna and mailing the driver tiny bits of it every day. No? Okay, so just the flicking him off part.

But here's the kicker: by eating meat you are actually causing more damage to the environment than that Hummer-driving moron. The only difference is if you buy a Hummer, you KNOW you're being an asshole.

Many meat-eaters and even vegetarians who eat dairy just don't know about the horrors of factory farming. In addition to being significantly damaging to the environment, the factory farming industry exploits cheap immigrant labor and provides a really nasty, contaminated product in the process.

Two Vegan Buzzkills Educate You So You Can Never Plead Ignorance on This Stuff Ever Again

We're about to lay down some hard-core facts for you that we found by reading reports, listening to scientists, and shutting out the trite, partisan, fact-free bullshit spewing from the television. None of this information came from TV news, but we've been reporting this stuff on *Citizen Radio* for years.

Working conditions at confined animal feeding operations (CAFOs) are unhealthy and extremely dangerous, and workers breathe in all kinds of harmful gases like ammonia, carbon dioxide, methane, and hydrogen sulfide. CAFO workers commonly complain of sinusitis, acute and chronic bronchitis, inflamed mucus membranes and irritation of the nose and throat, headaches, and muscle aches and pains.

Workers are expected to kill at extremely fast rates, and since the industry benefits the more carcasses it pumps out, all the incentives rest in speeding up the line and not protecting workers. Most slaughterhouses operate twenty-four hours a day, seven days a week.

According to a 2005 Human Rights Watch report, one worker phrased the experience of working in a kill line this way: "The line is so fast there is no time to sharpen the knife. The knife gets dull and you have to cut harder. That's when it really starts to hurt, and that's when you cut yourself."[12]

While it's difficult to know exactly how many workers are injured annually in slaughterhouse accidents—many workers are afraid to report injuries out of fear of losing their jobs (some due to being undocumented workers), and many corporations pay supervisors bonuses for minimizing worker-comp claims—we do know that the combination of long hours and repetitive motion leads to an increased risk of injury. It's not uncommon for a single worker to make up to forty thousand repetitive cuts in a single shift, and workers frequently report chronic pain in their hands, wrists, arms, shoulders, and backs.

Imagine working an eight-hour shift where not only are you responsible for making the same movement over and over and over again, but that movement results in killing a living creature with a dull knife. Over and over and over.

"The last hour of a regular shift is hard. You're tired and it's hard to concentrate. Then they tell you to work two hours overtime. That's when it gets downright dangerous," stated another employee in the HRW report.

A 2009 study from Amy J. Fitzgerald, of the University of Windsor, and Linda Kalof and Thomas Dietz, of Michigan State University, found that slaughterhouse employment increases total arrest rates, arrests for violent crimes, arrests for rape, and arrests for other sex offenses in comparison with other industries.[13]

The study found violent crimes including sexual assault and rape increase in towns once an abattoir moves in. Fitzgerald compared statistics from 581 counties in the United States to prove the link, and reported in her findings that laborers become desensitized to violence when they kill animals all day. She ruled out factors like influx of young men and immigrants, two factors frequently blamed for increases in violence.

"The unique thing about [abattoirs] is that [workers are] not dealing with inanimate objects, but instead dealing with live animals coming in and then killing them, and processing what's left of them," she said.

Similarly, a 2013 study published in *Society and Animals* found that Australian meat workers' aggression levels were "so high they're similar to the scores . . . for incarcerated populations."[14]

Not only is it superdangerous to work in the meatpacking industry, but it's also dangerous to eat the meat itself. And the beef industry had a collective epic freak-out when, referring to mad cow disease, talk show host Oprah Winfrey said on air in 1995, "It has just stopped me cold from eating another burger!"

The beef industry sued Oprah—*Oprah!* That's kind of like suing God. That's how powerful the beef industry is in the United States. They took God to court!

And all Oprah did was point out there's gross stuff in the meat, and she didn't even get into the hormones, chemicals, feces, and other bonus fun prizes in your McWhoppers.

Litigation dragged on for four years before a federal judge in Texas dismissed the absurd lawsuit that claimed Oprah violated the state's "veggie libel" law by maligning the beef industry. Yes, that's a real thing. Food libel laws, a.k.a. "veggie libel laws," are on the books in thirteen states (Alabama, Arizona, Colorado, Florida, Georgia, Idaho, Louisiana, Mississippi, North Dakota, Ohio, Oklahoma, South Dakota, and Texas) and make it easier for food producers to sue their critics for libel when they are merely stating true facts about the state of your meat.

Now, about your "organic" meat and eggs: We hate to be the ones to break it to you, but there is very little oversight and regulation when it comes to what is deemed an "organic" product and what's a regular ol' factory-farm meat slab. An organic label is no guarantee those animals were killed humanely (whatever that means—as if there's ever a humane way to kill a living creature) and most meat served at restaurants comes from factory farms.

The thing is, we know you aren't a monster. No one is sitting around, looking at a baby cow, and thinking, "I'm gonna skin and eat that cute little thing, and I hope when I eat it, there is shit in the meat and the immigrant who actually killed it is traumatized, and then the planet BURNS!" Most people are just ignorant and it's always easier to stay that way.

And it would be naive to hope the mainstream media plans to link the meat-and-climate-change issues for you, considering the fact that Al Gore is still kind of chubby and now, a word from our sponsors: Organic Valley Milk!

So since this is our book, and we run an independent podcast that doesn't bow to corporate interests, we're not afraid of grossing you out because you can't change the channel and lose us our sponsors. (Mostly because you already paid for the book and let's be honest, are you really going to waste gas driving to the bookstore to return it NOW? Because that's not only environmentally irresponsible, it's also probably going to cost you even more what with oil prices these days. Aaaaaaanyway.)

We actually mock other cultures for eating dog, but we chomp down on countless cows, an animal some cultures see as a GIFT FROM GOD. Some cultures eat horses and cats. We would never do that because we aren't savages! We just let baby male chicks suffocate in a pile of their dead brothers, skin cows alive, send female cows to "rape racks," all so we can drink a different species's milk, and put baby chickens in cages so small that their claws grow to wrap around the bars. But shame on those other uncivilized countries that eat the couple of animals we like.

Many professed outrage at cocktail parties around New York when Michael Vick tortured dogs, while eating tortured animals themselves in the canapés at said parties, which troubles us—and it should trouble you, too. It's time to be honest about where our food comes from, and how we determine what is "ethical" to eat.

(For legal reasons, we should probably point out here that we're not doctors, and we don't want to sound like creepy New Age self-help gurus [hence the copious amounts of profanity] but we have been vegan for a long time, so we'd like to pause, and focus on some more of the common myths and concerns associated with veganism.)

So Here Are Some Myths from Prime-Time Health and Environmental Reporting

Myth: Milk is good for you!

Truth: Actually, it's really fattening and filled with hormones, chemicals, and pus. Yup, you read that correctly. Pus! It's common for cows to experience painful inflammation in their mammary glands, and it's one of the most frequently cited reasons for sending cows to slaughter. There are about 150 bacteria, including E. coli, that cause this inflammation, but the symptoms aren't always visible, so milk's somatic cell count (SCC) is checked to determine if the milk is infected. Those somatic cells include white blood cells, a.k.a. "pus," and skin cells that are shed from the lining of the udder. The SCC of healthy milk is below 100,000 cells per milliliter, but—and here's the really important detail—the dairy industry is allowed to combine milk from all the cows in a herd in order to arrive at a "bulk tank" somatic cell count (BTSCC). Milk with a maximum BTSCC of 750,000 cells per milliliter can be sold. A BTSCC of 700,000 or more generally indicates that two-thirds of the cows in the herd are suffering from udder infections.

To make matters worse, some studies suggest milk *causes* osteoporosis, ironic given the decades-long marketing campaign insisting that milk improves bone strength. Studies have shown that cultures with much lower dairy intake rates than the US actually have better bone density.

In a paper published in the *Journal of the American Medical Association Pediatrics* in 2013, Harvard pediatrician David Ludwig points out that bone fracture rates tend to be lower in countries that do not consume milk.[15]

Likewise, in *The China Study*, T. Colin Campbell highlights a study that followed one thousand women 65 and older for seven years. Women with the highest ratio of animal to plant protein had 3.7 times more bone fractures and lost bone almost four times faster than women with the lowest ratios. Campbell points out that the women with the lowest ratios still consumed about half their total protein from animal sources. Rural China's ratio is about 10 percent animal to plant protein, and their fracture rate is one-fifth the US rate.[16]

Similar studies have been conducted within the United States. A University of California study showed that American women age

50 and over have one of the highest hip fracture rates in the world despite being some of the biggest drinkers of dairy.[17]

Additionally, a twelve-year Harvard Nurses' Health Study involving seventy-eight thousand nurses found that nurses who drank the most milk (two or more glasses per day) actually had a slightly higher risk of arm fracture (5 percent increase) and significantly higher risk of hip fracture (45 percent increase).[18]

And did we mention it's FATTENING? The reason those tiny cows latch onto their mommies' udders is so they can grow hundreds of pounds in very little time. We, as humans, do not need to gain hundreds of pounds that quickly. We are the only species that nibbles on boobies after infancy, and we're *certainly* the only species that sucks on ANOTHER SPECIES'S milk jugs after infancy. Those nips don't even belong to our moms. I mean, WHAT.

Myth: Milk is the only good source of calcium.

Truth: Actually, here's another source that doesn't involve crawling under a cow's udder and ingesting pus: eat some greens. Or drink almond milk. These sources have less fat, are less gross, and have plenty of calcium and protein.

Myth: I can only get my protein from dead animals.

Truth: You can get protein from a lot of sources that don't involve devouring a creature with parents. *Where do you get your protein?* This is the question vegans are asked the most, but usually we are too busy ruining your barbecue to answer, so here it is in print.

Tons of vegan foods have lots of protein: kale, broccoli, nuts, beans, chickpeas, tofu, tempeh, mushrooms, and more.

The difference is, with meat you are getting protein plus

cholesterol (and no fiber), and with veggies you are getting protein plus *no cholesterol* and *added fiber*.

So the next time a dude bro at the gym accusingly shouts, "Where do you get your protein, bro?!" you can tell him that. Or shout, "Your dad's cock!" and run away.

Your choice.

Myth: Carbohydrates are bad and I can never, ever eat them. If I can't have carbs, and I can't eat meat, won't I die?

Truth: Carbs are good! Any fad diet that tells you to eat bacon instead of fruit should have its creators charged with genocide. Carbs equal energy, and you need energy to do stuff like work out and live your life. If anyone tells you not to eat carbs, they are stupid. Now, with that said, there are good carbs and bad, starchy carbs, which is where our patented Kill Whitey! rule comes into play.

Don't eat white carbs: starchy pasta, white rice, and Wonder Bread. Always opt for brown rice, like a good little starter-vegan. Brown is always better than white. KILL WHITEY! If you can cook with quinoa, it's a great ricelike carb that is packed with protein. Quinoa pasta is also a thing and it's wonderful and it looks and tastes like regular pasta, but it's way healthier. The authors eat so much of it that one day we paused to check the ingredients to make sure it didn't say "Quinoa . . . and *meth*."

So those are just a few of the myths you won't see dispelled in the mainstream media when reporters and networks are chasing much bigger stories like the most recent elected official to put his penis in someone who is not his wife. And it's not just because we want to lure you to our own personal dark side that we've built an entire chapter around veganism. We're telling you what other news outlets won't—and it's all based in fact and reportage, just like their news—but we won't lose sponsors if we say "climate change" three times in a row on air and a vegan Beetlejuice will not appear to mock our listeners. But that would be cool.

Independent media is an essential tool to parse fact from fiction, and move past the culture wars, so listeners and viewers can finally—once and for all—learn the truth about the future of our planet.

Finally, the REAL reason you bought this book: a recipe from a high school dropout with no cooking experience!

Jamie's Vegan Better-Than-Stupid-Pad-Thai Pad Thai

1 package gluten-free brown rice pad thai/fettuccini

3 tablespoons natural almond butter

3 tablespoons rice wine vinegar

2 tablespoons low-sodium soy sauce or Bragg's

1–2 tablespoons agave

6 cloves garlic

A shit ton of green onions

Big ol' thing of broccoli

Sliced almonds *(optional)*

Bean sprouts *(optional)*

1. Boil a big-ass pot of water and follow the directions on the pasta package (usually cook and stir for 10 to 12 minutes after water is boiled and turn down to medium heat). Since no cookbooks told Jamie to turn the heat down after it boiled, he thought he would save you the countless bags of destroyed pasta he made.

2. In another pot, sauté the garlic and chopped, washed broccoli. When broccoli is starting to get soft, add the chopped green onions.

3. In a bowl, stir together the other ingredients until the almond butter is smooth (add a little water if you need to).
4. When everything is done, combine, stir the shit out of it, serve, garnish with almonds and bean sprouts, and EAT!

CHAPTER 4

Just Because You're Pro-Choice Doesn't Mean You're Not a Sexist Douche Bag

Still with us? Excellent!

The "War on Women" has been around for a long time, but it became a key aspect of the 2008 and 2012 campaign seasons, particularly as a hot-button issue on TV news programs and link bait for online journalists. All across the country, lawmakers—typically male lawmakers—were placing restrictions on women's health care and stripping protections for women and their families. These politicians restricted access to contraception, cut off funding for Planned Parenthood, mandated medically unnecessary ultrasounds, created abortion taxes and abortion waiting periods, forced women to tell their employers why they want birth control, and prohibited insurance companies from including abortion coverage in their policies.

More than fifty abortion clinics across the country have closed or stopped offering the procedure since these legislative attacks began in 2010, according to the *Huffington Post*'s nationwide survey of state health departments, abortion clinics, and local abortion-focused advocacy groups.[1]

Meanwhile, conservatives spread false information about women's reproductive health. During an appearance on MSNBC, Foster Friess, a prominent backer of Rick Santorum, expressed his confusion over this whole "contraceptive" business.[2]

"This contraceptive thing, my gosh, it's [so] inexpensive. Back in my days, they used Bayer Aspirin for contraceptives," he said.

What Friess meant was, if women held an aspirin between their legs, they couldn't open them far enough to get pregnant.

Just in case the American public didn't get the old and tired joke, he explained to a horrified Andrea Mitchell: "The gals put it between their knees, and it wasn't that costly."

Yet Mitchell didn't dispute the facts. She merely responded, "I'm just trying to catch my breath from that, Mr. Friess," and went on with the interview.

Todd Akin, a longtime antichoice activist and Republican representative from Missouri, was asked in an August 2012 interview with St. Louis television station KTVI-TV if women who are raped and become pregnant should have the option of abortion. His response was:

Well, you know, people always want to try to make that as one of those things, well how do you, how do you slice this particularly tough sort of ethical question. First of all, from what I understand from doctors, that's really rare. If it's a legitimate rape, the female body has ways to try to shut that whole thing down. But let's assume that maybe that didn't work or something. I think there should be some punishment, but the punishment ought to be on the rapist and not attacking the child.[3]

His comments led to uproar over the term "legitimate rape,"

and the idea that the magical uterus somehow has a way of differentiating between wanted and enemy sperm.

In all of the above instances, it's ironic that historically Big Gub'mint-averse Republicans are advocating for Big Brother to violate the privacy of citizens in the most invasive way imaginable, i.e., by hanging out in their vaginas.

It also raises the question: why does the media keep asking politicians questions about the medical health of women that politicians are not qualified to answer? This is a guaranteed way to spread falsehoods (see: aspirin between the knees, "legitimate rape"), which can only result in a misinformed public.

Sometimes the harassment of women came from the media itself. For example, radio host Rush Limbaugh labeled Georgetown Law student Sandra Fluke a "slut" because Fluke criticized the health insurance policies of her university, and claimed the school's lack of contraception coverage has a harmful impact on female students.

Fluke's big slutty move was saying, "I'm an American woman who uses contraceptives."

In Limbaugh's world, a woman who has bodily autonomy, and uses contraception responsibly is obviously a big ol' slut. (And if she didn't use birth control and got pregnant, then she'd be a welfare queen, but that's a separate incoherent rant for a separate incoherent day, right, Rush?)

Limbaugh later doubled down on the statement by claiming Fluke was asking the government to subsidize her sex life.

"What does that make her?" he asked. "It makes her a slut, right? It makes her a prostitute."

Then he upped the creep factor even more:

"If we are going to pay for your contraceptives, thus pay for you to have sex, we want something for it, and I'll tell you what it is: we want you to post the videos online so we can all watch."

For once, Republican politicians balked at the messaging of the longtime messiah of the right. House Speaker John Boehner called Limbaugh's comments "inappropriate," Rick Santorum said the radio host was "being absurd," and several advertisers ended up bailing on Limbaugh's show.

Limbaugh later apologized to Fluke in a written statement posted online in which he called his word choices "insulting," and on ABC's *The View* he apologized again in a super passive-aggressive way, saying he "acted too much like the leftists who despise me."

Much like with the issue of climate change (see chapter 3, "Al Gore Is Fat and We're All Going to Die"), the media doesn't serve to educate the public when it brings two ideologues on air to duke it out over the subject of women's health. Naturally, a Republican and a Democrat will have contrasting views on the hot-button issue of abortion, but in the same way that only a real scientist can reliably inform the audience about the effects of climate change, only a real doctor can tell the audience if these pre-abortion procedures invented by right-wing legislators are even *medically necessary*.

Republican lawmakers always claim the restrictions they place on women's reproductive health are for the woman's own good, but—!!!SPOILER ALERT!!!—usually that's not the case.

There is no evidence at all that the invasive vaginal ultrasound is a medical necessity, and in fact its only purpose is to place another hurdle between a woman and her doctor, and to scare her away from a common medical procedure.

According to a 2012 report published in *Perspectives on Sexual and Reproductive Health,* 87 percent of women were "highly confident" in their decisions before counseling ahead of an abortion procedure.[4]

But conservative (and largely male) lawmakers don't trust this scientific statistic, and so they craft restrictive policies designed to violate the will of women, and places like Fox News add confusion to the national debate by claiming the whole "War on Women" concept is phony and invented by Democrats.

We know you like direct quotes from assholes, so here are a few fun ones:

Fox's Laura Ingraham called it the "phony War on Women" that was "contrived" by Democrats.

Fox & Friends cohost Steve Doocy said he "completely agreed."

And Michelle Malkin concurred, saying the War on Women was "invented to take people's eyes off the prize, which is the economy."[5]

Because, you know, women's ability to control their reproductive status has nothing to do with the economy, or women's ability to work and contribute to said economy.

Worse, despite the fact that reproductive health care has undeniably been restricted, only 31 percent of women believe that there is currently a broad-based campaign to limit their access to reproductive health care, while 45 percent believe there are groups trying to limit women's reproductive health choices and services, but it is not a wide-scale effort, according to a 2012 survey conducted by the Henry J. Kaiser Family Foundation, a nonpartisan health care research organization.[6] Most women literally do not know that the War on Women is in fact real, and being waged against them.

The media has been complicit in allowing conservative ideologues to disseminate their damaging propaganda. And abortion rights are only one facet of this complicated, misogynistic, and not-ready-for-prime-time story.

The Time Jamie Went on TV to Say Rape Is Bad and America Exploded

On July 17, 2012, Jamie was invited on the *Melissa Harris-Perry Show* as part of a roundtable of comedians to discuss the fallout from Comedy Central star Daniel Tosh's recent encounter with a woman at a comedy club in L.A., in which he allegedly said to a female audience member that "it would be funny if five guys raped [you] right now."

You might be thinking, *Um . . . in what way is this comedy?*

Well, Jamie would agree with you, and he said as much on national television.

According to the recap given on *Melissa Harris-Perry*, what happened was that Tosh came out onstage and asked the audience, "So, what do you guys want to talk about tonight?" Apparently a man in the audience called out "Rape!" and Tosh began to run with that prompt under the (as he later claimed) auspices of "anything can be funny" until, moments later, a female audience member raised an objection, saying something to the effect that "rape is never funny." Tosh then proceeded with the witty comeback about five guys raping his heckler.

The MSNBC panel was convened not only to discuss the experience of being heckled and the issue of whether jokes about rape can ever be deemed "funny," but also as to what constitutes "free speech," which is what Tosh's vehement supporters used as their single loudest rallying cry when defending him.

It was a nuanced and spirited discussion among like-minded individuals, although some panelists were quicker than others to condemn Tosh (or at least that particular "joke"), some focused more on the rageful Tosh supporters, and Jamie—well, Jamie had the gumption to say the joke, or threat, or stupid comeback, or whatever it was, was just unacceptable any way you sliced it, regardless of politics or gender or free speech or being heckled or being a fellow comedian or having your own TV show.

And Jamie invoked the term "rape culture."

He thought the segment went well. He walked out of the studio, whistled a jaunty tune, and woke up the next morning to find thousands of messages like this in his Twitter feed: (TRIGGER WARNING!)

@jamiekilstein I'm going to rape you fucking homo.

OH! He calls Jamie gay AND wants to rape him? Progressive!

@jamiekilstein U mangina, ur just trying to get feminist pussy!

RIGHT! Because nothing gets the gals at the bar more hot and bothered than walking up to them and whispering, "Don't worry. I'm not going to rape you."

@jamiekilstein What happens if a girl cums when you rape them?

This was an actual message, like this guy thinks the girl should send the rapist a thank-you card for helping her achieve orgasm. Horrifically enough, many disturbed men think this way.

Most of these tweets would also "@" Tosh or other comedians, like the tweeters thought these comics would pause and think, "This random internet loser loves saying rape. *I* love saying rape. I should bring him on the road to open for me and we can say rape together!"

This went on for months. Threats and harassment, causing Jamie to cancel gigs and have panic attacks. Dudeman Jamie Kilstein almost, for a couple months, found out what it was like to be an average woman. Every time he logged on to Twitter, every time someone gave him a weird look on the subway, he would imagine a line of male cheerleaders waving pompons and spelling out "R-A-P-E C-U-L-T-U-R-E" before making a human pyramid of totally not funny rapists.

The weirdest part of this whole surreal scenario was that Jamie literally thought this was going to be the *least* controversial thing he has ever said! He's gone on TV and said there is no God. He thought he might lose everything after that. But nope. Just a couple of upset tweets insisting, "Yes there is!"

He talked about drone strikes on *Conan*, and while there were a lot of angry comments on *Conan*'s Facebook page, and he was never invited back (more on that in chapter 8), the response paled in comparison to the MSNBC incident. He said rape culture is bad, clapped his hands together, and the internet exploded. Bros everywhere: "DON'T TALK ABOUT RAPE, THAT'S MY GAME!" It was like a bat signal went out, but instead of a bat, it was a TapouT shirt, and rape sympathizers everywhere assembled online.

Even fellow comics rallied to defend rape jokes. Alternative comics and mainstream comics, maybe for the first time ever, united to say: "Hey, rape is super funny." Now, it's important to remember that *comics don't agree on anything*. They don't band together. They don't even have health insurance or a union. But *this* was their calling—the hill they would die on. The hill of rape jokes.

The saddest hill in all the land.

Jamie would turn to Allison, who as a journalist and lady on the internet, gets this shit every day, and yell, "What's wrong with people?! Rape threats?? What is the world coming to? When did this start?! WITH ME? Am I the first??"

And Allison would very nicely close her browser with all of her rape threats for the day and say, "I don't know, champ. You gonna be okay?"

See, a lot of people assume that because women can legally drive and express their beliefs in public that the fight for equality has been won. If you listen very carefully right now, you can probably hear the distant, lone cry of some angry white male: "Just let them vote and paint their nails, so they'll shut up!" Or folks might assume that once women actually make as much money doing the same job as men (according to the US Census Bureau, women would need an average of a 65 percent pay increase to catch up to their male counterparts), it will mean true equality for 50 percent of the world's population.

The truth is, the fight for real equality is much more elusive and complicated, and women are still routinely treated as subhuman, second-class citizens as a by-product of this thing called rape culture.

But that's not something you see on major news networks like CNN or Fox News, even though rape culture is everywhere. It's in the way women are exploited by mass marketing campaigns as sex objects or pleasurable snacks to be consumed the way men would eat beef jerky. It's in the way women are consistently portrayed as being shrill and humorless in the comedy community for demanding things like equal rights and dignity. It's in the way a woman is a prude if she doesn't put out, and a slut if she's sexually independent. It's in the way women earn less than men for doing the same job, and issues like rape and sex trafficking remain underreported epidemics that governments have yet to get serious about addressing, but these same officials *are* willing to crack down on consensual transactions between sex workers and their clients.

What We Talk About When We Talk About Rape Culture (in the Media)

CNN gave a clinic in how to facilitate rape culture during its coverage of the Steubenville, Ohio, rape of a young woman by two local football stars. CNN anchor Poppy Harlow expressed concern, not for the rape survivor, but for the *rapists*. "It was incredibly emotional, it was difficult for anyone in there to watch those boys break down," Harlow said after the network played footage from the courtroom. As an afterthought, she added: "[It was] also difficult, of course, for the victim's family."[7]

Harlow starred in another #newsfail alongside anchor Candy Crowley when both women lamented the lost promise of the two rapists.

Harlow again set up the segment by describing it as "incredibly difficult" to watch. "These two young men, who had such promising futures, star football players, very good students, literally watched as they believed their [lives] fell apart."

Doubling down, Crowley then asked CNN legal analyst Paul Callan: "What's the lasting effect, though, on two young men being found guilty in juvenile court of rape essentially?"[8]

Will they ever be able to rape again? Think of the children!

Harlow was roundly critiqued for this coverage and one CNN insider said, "Poppy is taking this extremely personally as a woman. She's outraged that someone would think she'd do such a thing [as slant her coverage toward rapists]. It's gotten so out of control."

So, did Poppy Harlow wake up one morning and think: *Gee, I think I'll slant my coverage to sympathize with rapists today?* Of course not. But that's the thing about rape culture—it's *part* of our day-to-day culture. And individuals are not immune to participating in rape culture simply because they're women. As Harlow and Crowley ably demonstrated, women can blame and shame other women with the best of them.

(To any bros reading this: don't strain any muscles rolling your eyes or throwing your beer bong against the fraternity's common space wall. Rape culture is real. It is a thing. We have even more proof! Whether we're talking about the media failing to cover horrific rape cases because outlets don't consider rape culture newsworthy; the latest lazy rape joke at a comedy club; or Missouri representative Todd Akin's theory about magical ovaries rejecting the sperm of "legitimate" rapists; or Paul Ryan saying "rape is a method of conception"—rape culture is everywhere.)

Take, for example, the media's very different coverage of the Penn State sex abuse scandal and the suicide of Lizzy Seeberg, a student at Saint Mary's College, who took her life after her claims of being assaulted in a dorm room by two Notre Dame football players were met with threats and indifference. As Dave Zirin writes at *The Nation*, allegations that revered assistant coach Jerry Sandusky raped young boys were taken gravely seriously by the sports world and general media, whereas the rape of a young woman, and her eventual suicide, were met with a collective yawn.

Zirin pontificates about why the two stories were handled so differently within the media and concludes: "The only answer that makes sense is that raping women has become 'normalized' in our culture, while raping little boys has not. The only answer that makes sense is that the rape of a young boy sets all sorts of alarms of horror in the minds of the very male sports media, while the rape of women does not. The only answer that makes sense is that it's been internalized that while boys are helpless in the face of a predator, women are responsible for their assault. The accusers are the accused."[9]

Even when rape culture is discussed more broadly in the media—as with the Tosh scandal—women are usually framed as being too sensitive about the whole penetration-against-their-will thing.

When Daniel Tosh told a girl at a comedy club that "it would be funny if five guys raped [you] right now," and she walked out trembling, men everywhere took to the internets and started typing frantically like little rapey hackers, not to defend the girl, of course, for these are the kinds of nerds who screamed unironically in all-caps lock that this girl was TOTALLY ASKING FOR IT by telling Tosh that she didn't think rape was funny. You see, Tosh, who bunked down in his giant pile of Comedy Central cash after the incident, and who subsequently secured a *second* show on the network, is BEING CENSORED!

The absolute best responses from Tosh groupies following this incident were the far-fetched hypothetical situations that COULD have, but would never ACTUALLY have, happened at the club.

A general example: "What if Tosh said, 'I hope you get attacked by a dog that knows karate,' and that girl was attacked by a dog who knows karate?! WOULD THAT HAVE BEEN HIS FAULT TOO?!?!"

Okay, first of all, has that ever happened? Ever? In the history of the world?

And second: If it did, are one in four girls attacked by karate dogs? If they were attacked, would people ask the survivor if she was drinking with the karate dog, or if she has a sexual history with dogs who know karate? Would they ask her if she was carrying a Frisbee that night, or if she'd rubbed dog food all over her face? Had she insulted the dog's karate master? What do you think is going to happen when you're hanging out after dark AT THE POUND?

No? None of that happened? Oh. Maybe it's because the hypothetical question was fucking stupid.

Not only do rape survivors and women in general have to deal with being the victims of a violent crime, but then they have to deal with the added burden of living in a culture that mocks, trivializes, and often denies the existence of the crime itself, or blames the survivor for courting her attack.

If your car was stolen and you walked all the way back home, only to turn on the TV and see Candy Crowley say, "Another dumb idiot, who was asking for it, had their car stolen today," you would probably be pretty bummed out. Now, imagine instead of your car being stolen, someone had sex with you against your will.

That is rape culture.

Get it?

You Should Be Able to Tell the Difference Between the Media and Your Uninformed, Drunk Uncle

It shows how accustomed to rape culture Americans have become that so few people made the connection between stuff like rape jokes and Todd Akin, but the reason comics feel they can get away with making jokes about forcible penetration and that an elected official believes in ovarian faeries combating rapists' semen is precisely because of rape culture.

Sexist rhetoric, rather than being the ammunition of fringe lunatics, is frequently utilized by mainstream figures. Pat Robertson, conservative television evangelist and cofounder of the Christian Coalition, once told a woman concerned about the dalliances of her flirtatious husband, to "make herself as attractive as possible" to stop his eye from wandering, and "not hassle him" about it.[10]

It's easy for good liberal guys to look at an old coot like Pat and laugh at him, but many of them have said similar things to their friends, and their "joking" statements start to be received as accepted, normal conversation.

By the way, this isn't an out-of-the-ordinary comment for Pat. He once said, "The feminist agenda is not about equal rights for women," but is rather "a socialist, anti-family political movement that encourages women to leave their husbands, kill their children, practice witchcraft, destroy capitalism and become lesbians." When discussing the proper role of a wife, Robertson said, "Christ is the head of the household and the husband is the head of the wife, and that's the way it is, period."[11]

In Pat's world, Jesus is at the head of the dinner table, asking the kids how school was. Meanwhile, Gloria Steinem is outside leading a gang bang with the Jews while casting spells on Christian children.

This isn't to say that the men acting as apologists or enablers for figures like Pat or Todd Akin—or any other politician who's been invited on air to spew lies and malice into the homes of the viewing/voting public—are stupid (okay, some of them are stupid), but more often the explanation is that rape culture is so prevalent that some men can't even see it, so they accuse feminists of making it up! Just like women made up the "clit" and the female orgasm.

And the problem extends beyond religious zealots. In addition to bigoted pundits disseminating misinformation into the general populace, sometimes the media excludes women from the conversation almost entirely.

In February 2012, Congress received widespread criticism for convening an all-male panel to discuss birth control, and rejected a woman who attempted to testify. But as Fairness & Accuracy in Reporting (FAIR) notes, the next day, a males-only panel appeared on MSNBC's *Morning Joe* to (unironically) chat about how terrible it was that an all-male panel was permitted to discuss women's reproductive rights.[12]

Women can't get in on the conversation anywhere, it seems.

A *ThinkProgress* study found that in a four-day period in February 2012, men constituted 62 percent of the guests on cable networks who commented on birth control. In the February 12 episode of NBC's *Meet the Press*, only one female remarked on the contraception story, out of six total guests and the male host.[13]

And the #newsfail is even worse when it comes to women of color, who have higher rates of unintended pregnancies and have less access to affordable birth control. When a woman does manage to sneak her way onto a media panel, she is almost always a white woman.

Back in Washington, misogynist fools have a lot of help from their GOP brethren and rape culture to pave the way for their dangerous statements, and then the media invites them on to make sure America is paying attention.

When Akin made the "legitimate rape" remark, what he was essentially arguing is that there is such a thing as "real rape" and "fake rape." The real rape is done by scary poor, black men brandishing AK-47s in an alley. Oh, and also the survivor is white, and probably blond.

Saying "legitimate rape" implies that very real stuff (put your beers down, bros) like date rape and spousal rape don't count. Sorry, ladies. We know you felt like that date-turned-rape was the worst moment of your life, but actually, you shouldn't have been drinking, or wearing that outfit, and you certainly shouldn't have trusted your date, so this one is on you.

Allowing pundits to repeat messaging like "legitimate rape" on the news conditions impressionable people in the same way the GOP has long employed the "southern strategy" (a term that refers to Richard Nixon's plan to win white, southern voters by using coded racial language). It's also how the Bush administration used "shock and awe" and "Swiftboat" as shorthand to drill into the American people's minds the things they most wanted imprinted there, to the detriment of truth and facts.

These political tactics are well documented and undeniable, and it's high time that the mainstream media recognized that in their zest for "balanced" coverage they are giving a bullhorn to the same kind of dangerous, irresponsible, but easily digested nuggets of hate, deceit, and power-mongering that sometimes go by the term "propaganda."

The media shouldn't be in the business of brainwashing people.

So why is it so hard to report responsibly about things like the Steubenville and Maryville cases, high incidents of rape by collegiate and professional athletes, birth control, the repealing of reproductive health care laws, abortion patient harassment, and abortion provider assassinations—not to mention begin to report on the hundreds (thousands?) of cases each year that don't even make it to the local headlines, let alone the national stage? Well, first of all, it's not considered good "news." And it's a vicious cycle, because when the public doesn't hear much about rape, they don't think of it as a serious problem. And they assume guys like Todd Akin have a point when they minimize rape, and they elect men like him to enact laws, like those affecting abortion rights, to further victimize a large segment of the population (i.e., women and rape victims).

You know what the public has heard a lot about in recent years? Swine flu. In 2009, some media outlets were predicting H1N1 could kill up to 120 million people, and the London *Metro* even included that prediction over a picture of Mexican police with masks and machine guns.

Even though the White House clearly stated these high fatality figures represented "a possibility, not a prediction," *USA Today* ran the headline: "U.S. Report Predicts 30,000 to 90,000 H1N1 Deaths."

CNN dispensed with the low-end fatality figures and peddled the possibility that the United States could see "up to 90,000 deaths," according to the *Columbia Journalism Review*.

The New York *Daily News* and *New York Post* treated the story in similar fashions, and also used the word "predicted."[14]

The media loves the possibility of a pandemic because it's a terrifying story that guarantees audience attention. Meanwhile, the rape culture pandemic carries on without the same degree of media attention because, unlike H1N1, the patriarchy is nothing new. It's part of society's fabric that the media accepts as inevitable—barely newsworthy at all.

Don't Worry, Feminists Don't Want to Cut Off Your Penis; They Just Want Equality

Perhaps the fear held by some men is that Nazi feminists will set up gulags and gradually, man by man, try the entire male population for acts of rape. Naturally, trials will be determined by "feelings" and the presiding judge will be whoever is on her period at the time.

In reality, what most feminists (women and men) want is a civilized conversation about rape culture. We're not talking about forced castrations or man-shaming, or any of that bullshit. Men can be awesome feminist allies as soon as they let go of their egos and consider that they, by being men, are inherently born into privilege, and they simply can't fully empathize with what it's like to be a woman born into a world where the odds of sexual violence and discrimination are automatically stacked against you.

When conservative politicians attempt to categorize rape as being "real" or "legitimate," what they are essentially doing is believing the best of men and the worst of women.

Women are lying temptresses consumed by wedding fantasies and the desire to attract hapless men to the honeypots between their thighs and then BAM! they ensnare a husband. For example—and we swear, this is the only *Twilight* reference in this book—Kristen Stewart did what most twenty-two-year-olds do: be a jerk and mess up a relationship that wasn't going to last anyway. She cheated, and the world collectively lost its mind. She received death threats, lost work, and at the time of this writing, is enjoying being the spokesmodel for many slut-shaming campaigns. Conversely, Chris Brown beat the crap out of his girlfriend and was rewarded with Grammys; Charlie Sheen abuses women and gets a show on FX; and Ashton

Kutcher cheats and gets Charlie's old show! It's the circle of being the worst.

While the instances of men being falsely accused of rape are tragic (each and every one of them), as a collective problem, false accusations of rape pale in comparison to the issue of rape itself. Rape is a huge problem as it's documented right now, and assaults are extremely underreported. According to the Rape, Abuse & Incest National Network (RAINN), 54 percent of sexual assaults are not reported to the police, and 97 percent of rapists will never spend a day in jail.[15]

One of the reasons 54 percent of rapes are not reported is that when rape survivors hear people like Candy Crowley and Poppy Harlow defending rapists on the news, a part of them thinks: *Maybe it's my fault* or *I know it's not my fault, but I can't handle being discussed on national TV as though it is*, and then they don't report it.

If CNN is supposed to be a source of objective news, and "objective journalists" not only pardon rapists for their crimes, but also invite know-nothing conservatives onto their airwaves to spout ridiculous falsehoods about women and their bodies, then of course rape survivors become miseducated and self-blaming.

On *Citizen Radio*, we have this crazy idea that America should trust women.

When Lindy West, staff writer at *Jezebel*, was getting all kinds of harassment after her FX debate with comic Jim Norton, which was about if rape jokes are funny and whether criticism is the same thing as censorship (spoiler: it's not), we invited West on to talk about rape culture and rape jokes.

On *CR* we discussed that criticism is not the same thing as censorship. For example, Daniel Tosh has the right, and freedom, to say whatever he wants. The First Amendment protects that, but freedom of speech works both ways. Just as Tosh has the right to make rape jokes if that's his bag, Lindy West, and *Citizen Radio*, and a whole bunch of other activists have the right to talk back and say, *Hey, you're an asshole*. Furthermore, Tosh's speech is in no way restricted by the blowback he's received over his rape joke. He still has a show on Comedy Central. In fact, now he has *two* shows, so don't worry, bros. Tosh's speech is still fully protected.

Because we're not a news outlet that is consumed by a financially motivated desire to reinforce the culture wars, we were able to do an interview with a feminist who is also a comedy fan! Imagine that. Take *that*, stereotypes!

On *Citizen Radio*, we understand that only two things matter in the reproductive health debate: the medical opinions of doctors, and the will of women.

We also understand that feminism is intricately connected with all aspects of our society, including health, but also labor and the economy. A woman can't be an equal player in our society until she has total autonomy, and that includes determining the destiny of her own body.

That's the core of the gender equality debate.

Anything else is just #newsfail.

CHAPTER 5

The Gay Agenda

We all know the story: Old-man farmer in Iowa has been married to high school sweetheart for forty years. They have three kids, a dog named Patches, and a lifetime of precious memories.

One day, he looks up at the TV, and sees that gay people can now legally marry in his home state. He pauses to ponder that. Wistfully, he considers the life he has built for himself. He looks at Patches, curled up by the fire, looks at his little grandson, who is tinkering on his iPad. Already so grown up.

Then he looks at his wife, stands, fetches his overcoat, and shoves her out the front door as hard as he can, screaming, "SO LONG, HAG! IT'S GAY SEX TIME!"

He slams the door and proceeds to turn the farm into an all-male hand-job factory.

We've seen it a thousand times. Behold! The future of straight people if the gays marry!

The authors are quite obviously mocking such a ridiculous belief system. However, the beauty of living in the United States of

America is that you can believe whatever you want and live your life accordingly in a free state. What you can't do is pass legislation predicated upon beliefs (yours or anyone else's) that run counter to, you know, civil rights 'n' stuff.

It's easy to go after Republican lawmakers for being assholes because they can be SUCH assholes. Some of them are bigots who use a very outdated, potentially made-up book for "research" like others use Wikipedia. Some of them know better when it comes to LGBT rights, but they also have a very homophobic base they cater to, which means Prop 8! And some of them may harbor fantasies of farmside hand jobs themselves . . . but that's neither here nor there.

The bottom line is that politicians on both sides of the aisle, even many Democrats like President Obama, are wishy-washy when it comes to expressing clear and unadulterated support for gay rights.

It's like US politicians can't just say, "I support equal rights" without adding, "but only if that's cool with Jesus."

It's all well and good to hold old coots like Fred Phelps accountable, and let's be honest, it's fun to besmirch extremists like him on Twitter because (a) you get lots of retweets, but also (b) who is going to disagree with you? Fred Phelps? He doesn't know how to use Twitter! God? He's not real. It's win-win!

But when the politicians you vote for say anything other than, "Do I think same-sex marriage will affect heterosexual marriage? No, because I'm a fucking grown-up," that's a problem. Again, it doesn't matter what anyone personally believes about the issue of same-sex marriage—what matters is that in the eyes of the *law* we are all equal.

Interestingly, the majority of Americans agree with the authors on this one. According to a 2013 Gallup poll, 52 percent of respondents said they would support a law that would legalize same-sex marriage across all fifty states.[1] Yet the media continues to artificially stoke debate by inviting people like right-wing darling Bryan Fischer from the American Family Association on their airwaves to discuss the issue of same-sex marriage, as though he represents anyone but an aging, dying minority.

Fischer is the guy who complained that the Congressional Medal of Honor was "feminized" because it is often awarded for saving a life instead of killing the enemy, and that President Obama "wants Indian tribes to be our new overlords," and, following the Fort Hood shooting, argued that Muslims should be banned from serving in the US military.[2]

In other words, he is the perfect player for a media obsessed with preserving the culture wars instead of engaging in nuanced debate.

Is this really the best use of the media's time?

While Politicians Prayed, the Gay Community Got Shit Done

As fringe lunatics like Fischer occupied their prime-time news, activists recognized early on that change wasn't going to be disseminated from above by a benevolent Wolf Blitzer. Rather, change was going to come from the ground and trickle up.

It wasn't that long ago that Republicans were fantasizing about sending all gay people to their own planet: a sexy, sexy planet. But now, we have John McCain's daughter, Meghan, pressuring her dad to support LGBT rights, and little Joey Biden doing the same thing with President Obama. The gay community serves as a model for how direct action kicks ass and gets shit done, and they've made gains previously thought impossible in the last few decades alone. But it's essential we keep our eyes on the prize, which is full equality and protection under the law.

Of course, it's important to savor the victories. As of this writing, seventeen states and Washington, DC, have legalized same-sex marriage, Rhode Island recognizes same-sex marriages from other jurisdictions, and California recognizes them on conditional bases. Same-sex marriage was even briefly legal in Utah until January 2014, when the Supreme Court put a stay on the decision pending the state's appeal. In an unprecedented move, Attorney General Eric Holder intervened in the legal battle in Utah and announced the same-sex marriages that took place in that state are considered legal under federal law even though state officials will not recognize those unions.[3]

And back in 2011, President Obama brought to an end the discriminating policy "Don't Ask, Don't Tell," which barred gays from serving openly in the military.

The fact that this country, which has waged two occupations and countless military operations since 2001, finally said that anyone who wants to fight can fight regardless of who gets them horny, is pretty mind-blowing. There were men and women trapped in a desert overseas, not knowing if they would make it home, and they couldn't even have photos of their loved ones displayed publicly to get them through the ordeal. That is shameful, and what's worse is it took the media a long time to expand their gay rights coverage beyond the issue of same-sex marriage.

But even when the media finally weighed in on the highly problematic program "Don't Ask Don't Tell," they largely excluded the people most affected by the policy: LGBT individuals.

Following the repeal of DADT, only three of twenty-five sources commenting on DADT on ABC, CBS, and NBC—one on each network—identified as gay, lesbian, bisexual, or transgender, or was representing an LGBT organization.[4]

And as Fairness & Accuracy in Reporting notes, these stories weren't about the discriminatory nature of DADT, but rather a debate about the "timing" being wrong to repeal the policy, and how rolling back the program would undermine "military cohesion."

Once again, human rights took a backseat to partisan bickering. And if the "media experts," i.e., "entrenched hacks," actually bothered to listen to the real experts, they could have quickly learned DADT was terrible for military cohesion.

Author Nathaniel Frank conducted many interviews with gay and lesbian soldiers, and demonstrated that it's not being gay that makes things weird in the barracks, but the fact that the LGBT soldiers so feared their secrets being revealed and getting kicked out of the military that they distanced themselves from their unit, thereby causing tension. The times when their sexualities were made common knowledge, everything was fine because—surprise!—gay people can get along with their fellow human beings and accomplish tasks even when in the company of the same sex just fine, thank you very much.[5]

So there were these studies rolling out showing that Don't Ask, Don't Tell actually *harms* camaraderie within the military, there were more US-led invasions and occupations going on than most Americans can keep track of, plus the majority of the country wanted an end to DADT because the two occupations in the Middle East needed all the help they could get, and it STILL took until 2012 to get rid of DADT because we needed to make sure we didn't alienate the "Never served in the military, but has his

'Support the Troops' bumper sticker on his gas-guzzling SUV and gay people make him nervous" constituency.

It's essential to remember that the LGBT community achieved these victories even when the federal government shunned them, and so-called allies burned them by signing damaging legislation like the Defense of Marriage Act (DOMA) signed by President Clinton (yes, the guy you always say you miss and who played the sax on *Arsenio*), which forbid the federal government from recognizing same-sex marriage, and which has now been declared unconstitutional in eight federal courts, including two federal appeals courts.

Dealing with mainstream Democratic politicians like Clinton has become something of a Sisyphean burden for the gay community. Time and time again, they throw their support behind a candidate who provides lukewarm acceptance of their existences because the other side, the Republican and now Tea Party side, is so abhorrent and bigoted. Who would you choose: a "compromise guy" or a "you and your loved ones will burn in a lake of fire, which I totally believe is a real thing" guy? The strategy to choose the lesser of two evils makes sense until it doesn't, and suddenly a Democratic president is the one solidifying law to universally declare your marriage illegitimate, and whose version of "compromise" looks like gays having to serve in secret in the military.

As usual, the American people were way ahead of the media on the issue of same-sex marriage and repealing DADT, but because the media is obsessed with preserving the culture wars, it continued to refer to DADT as a "divisive" issue even when it really wasn't.

In a 2010 *New York Times* article, Michael Shear wrote:

> But as the first full week of the 2010 general election season opens across the country on Monday, Washington is scheduled

once again to debate immigration and gay men, lesbians and bisexuals in the military, two deeply divisive social issues that threaten to polarize the conversation on the campaign trail.[6]

Back in 2010, 75 percent of Americans (and a majority of conservatives, Republicans, and evangelicals) agreed with lifting the ban. Those are hardly "divisive" numbers. If anything, it appeared as though Americans had already reached a consensus, but the media was late (as usual) to the game.

Yet outlets like CNN continued to reinforce the illusion of division when they aired "face-offs" between advocates and opponents of repealing the policy, again giving the impression that the country itself was evenly divided on the issue, even though that wasn't the case.

FAIR notes that CNN brought on Tony Perkins of the Family Research Council *twice* (once on *Larry King*, and another time on *Newsroom*) after he put out a press statement saying a repeal would "jeopardize our nation's security to advance the agenda of the radical homosexual lobby."[7]

Perkins' FRC colleague Peter Sprigg was also invited on Chris Matthews' MSNBC show, where he warned that repealing DADT was "guaranteed" to lead to sexual assault.

"If we had a policy where people were considered bigoted if they were opposed to same-sex conduct, then there would be much greater danger of misconduct on the part of the homosexuals," he argued.[8]

Scientific reasoning if we've ever heard it!

The false balance continues to this day. When the American Academy of Pediatrics in 2013 declared its support for marriage equality as being "in the best interests of children," CNN invited three panelists to discuss the story, including Reihan Salam of the right-wing *National Review* and Peter Sprigg (ugh) of FRC.

AAP might have based its position on more than thirty years of research, evaluated over a four-year period, but why should that matter when Sprigg has a hunch that gays are trying to brainwash the childrens?

CNN host Erin Burnett asked Sprigg (who is trained in ministry, not child psychology): "Is [the AAP] wrong?"

But the real question is: why is CNN asking uninformed bigots their opinions in order to skew the debate?

Who Needs Equality
When You Can Have False Equivalency?

Listen, we think it's terrific you watch *Glee* and feel, in a totally sincere and inspired way, vast quantities of compassion and love for Kurt Hummel. We love Kurt, too. WE LOVE YOU, KURT.

See?

But . . . here's the thing: just because you like *Glee*, and of course by extension support same-sex marriage and adoption (because you should totally support those things because it's 2014), there's something we need to tell you, fellow progressive: same-sex marriage is only one piece of equality for the LGBT community.

We get it. Because the media largely limits its coverage of LGBT rights to the issue of marriage, you may not know that. When was the last time you saw a discussion of trans rights in prime time (not counting Piers Morgan misgendering Janet Mock)?

The media's job is to serve as society's referee, throwing down objective truth flags when uninformed bigots are shouting their opinions into the wind. The questions the media should answer are: Will repealing DADT hurt troop morale? (No.) Will same-sex marriage lead to the downfall of society? (No.)

It is not the media's job to give platforms to members on the other side of a one-sided debate. If anything, doing so clouds the truth and makes it more difficult for the public to make informed decisions.

Because the media is stuck in this loop of endlessly playing out the culture wars, they limit their LGBT coverage to issues of marriage even though that's a very small part of the fight for equality.

Did you know, for example, that in twenty-nine states, employers can fire their workers for being gay? And that transgender people can be legally fired in thirty-three states?[9]

According to a study from the Anti-Violence Project (AVP), 40 percent of anti-LGBT murder victims in 2011 were transgender women even though transgender women make up only 10 percent of anti-LGBT violence survivors. Furthermore, transgender people of color were 28 percent more likely to experience physical violence compared to the rest of the sample of LGBT and HIV-affected people.[10]

But look, the authors are not here to teach Trans Rights 101. Neither is Allison or Jamie qualified to educate the American people on sodomy laws.

Ahem.

But what we can do is offer independent, unbiased coverage of the issues. And by "unbiased" we mean "truthful" because obviously we are biased . . . toward the truth! Whereas media executives who depend on advertising dollars to make their budgets and ratings to fatten up their annual bonuses are sometimes a little less concerned with the truth and a little more concerned with the logistics of getting a donkey and an elephant to mud-wrestle on air. Preferably a cute female elephant in a red power suit.

These executives are obsessed with creating "balance" to the detriment of "accurate reporting." Where, we ask, is the balance between granting basic civil rights to everyone in America under federal law and . . . not granting them to some people? Why should anyone arguing against granting civil rights to everyone in America *ever* be allowed on a news program to promote their opinion? There are reality shows for that kind of thing! And *The 700 Club*!

This is what the media thinks of you, middle America. You're idiots. And some of you . . . totally are. But most of you are victims of what Noam Chomsky calls "manufactured consent" because you've been force-fed a pro-war corporate agenda your entire lives. If the national news media broadcast into 99 percent of your homes day and night were in the business of truth-telling, most of you *would* be against wars and bank bailouts and realize how the fight for LGBT rights mirrors the struggle for the rights of women and people of color. But instead you are getting "fair and balanced" coverage and you are taking those "facts" to heart and using them when deciding which politicians to elect and send to Washington to pass laws that harm your fellow citizens.

The Media Looks Beyond Same-Sex Marriage . . . and Continues to Bring the Fail

In addition to peddling archaic balance standards, the media also has a disturbing tendency to put the onus of hate crime attacks on the victims.

For example, in 2012, a study was published in *Pediatrics*, the official journal of the American Academy of Pediatrics, that examined gender conformity in children and risk factors for abuse.

Here are a sampling of the headlines the media used to frame the study:

CNN: "KIDS WHO VEER FROM GENDER NORMS AT HIGHER RISK FOR ABUSE"

U.S. NEWS & WORLD REPORT: "GENDER IDENTITY ISSUES CAN HARM KIDS' MENTAL HEALTH"

ABC: "GENDER-NONCONFORMING STUDENTS AT ELEVATED RISK FOR ABUSE, POST-TRAUMATIC STRESS"[11]

Aside from conflating being transgender and being gender-nonconforming with veering from "gender norms," the headlines also assign the blame for abuse on the gender-nonconforming kids themselves. Being transgender is not "risky behavior," but what is risky is allowing bullies and attackers to get away with their crimes because they choose to target individuals labeled as deviant by the establishment media.

Then there was Chelsea Manning. Good times! When the whistle-blower announced her true gender, the establishment media collectively lost its mind, and then proceeded to handle the story in the clumsiest, most insulting way possible.

And look, whatever you may make of Chelsea Manning's alleged legal transgressions, that has nothing to do with her gender. Gender rights are separate from any political debate, just as we agree prisoners have the right not to be beaten and raped even if they might have committed very serious crimes. In a civilized society, we should respect the human rights of even our worst political opponents.

First, many major outlets refused to use the correct "she" pronoun when discussing Manning. CNN's Jake Tapper explained the network would be referring to Chelsea by her dead name, Bradley, and using male pronouns until such a time as her name is officially changed and her physical transition process has begun. NPR made a similar decision. Yet these outlets have no problem using names like "Madonna," "Bono," or "Meat Loaf."

CNN host Fredricka Whitfield, as of this writing, continues to incorrectly refer to Chelsea as a male, and during an August 24, 2013, edition of *Newsroom*, one of Whitfield's guests, criminal defense attorney Richard Herman, a regular CNN legal commentator, railed against the possibility of providing Manning with adequate medical care for her gender dysphoria with hormone treatments. He called the idea "beyond insanity," and suggested Manning could get "good practice" presenting as a female in prison:

> It's absurd. Sometimes we have to step back and say, "you know, some of these cases we cover, this is beyond insanity." There's no way that taxpayers are going to pay a hundred thousand dollars for a gender transformation for this guy while he's in prison. If he wants to be Chelsea, he can practice all he wants at Fort Leavenworth, because those guys are there for a long time. So he can get good practice and when he gets out, he can have the operation or whatever, and he can pay for it.[12]

In its initial coverage, the *New York Times* reported on Manning's press release using the wrong name and pronouns throughout the article, but then published a follow-up quoting *Times* managing editor Dean Baquet, saying:

> Generally speaking we call people by their new name when they ask us to, and when they actually begin their new lives. In this case we made the judgment readers would be totally confused if we turned on a dime overnight and changed the name and gender of a person in the middle of a major running news story. That's not a political decision. It is one aimed at our primary constituency— our readers.[13]

Deputy editor Susan Wessling embraced the same low opinion of readers: "We can't just spring a new name and a new pronoun [on readers with no explanation]."[14]

But no one was suggesting the *Times* present the new name and pronouns *without explanation*. Supporters of Chelsea Manning and transgender rights simply pointed out that refusing to acknowledge Manning's name and gender was an ignorant, bigoted decision on the parts of major outlets like CNN and the *Times*.

As of August 2013, the *Times* now uses "Chelsea" and "she" when discussing Manning.

As usual, MSNBC's *Morning Joe* managed to make both the *Times* and CNN looks like bastions of progressivism when substitute host Nicole Wallace conflated mental illness with gender identity and remarked, "Well, he's obviously a troubled person."[15]

The *troubled person* theme ran deep, even among so-called progressives.

Joy Reid, a pundit regularly featured and now a host on MSNBC, characterized Manning's announcement as "TMI," and wrote Manning is "a guy seeking anarchy as a salve for his own personal, psychological torment."[16]

The Daily Beast's editor Tina Brown hand-selected a column by former newspaper editor and ex-con Mansfield Frazier entitled "How Will Chelsea Manning Be Treated in Prison?" that contained a slew of factual inaccuracies. The article opens with a lengthy editor's note, which explains that while the column asserts "prison rape is rare," it is, in fact, not, because "200,000 adults and children are sexually abused in American detention facilities every year," and then quickly segues anyway into a bizarre defense of prison rape.[17]

Frazier states that Manning's experience "could be terrible," but "transgender and gay inmates are often treated quite well," which simply isn't true. A 2012 Department of Justice report confirmed that LGBT people face extremely high rates of sexual abuse, with more than one in three transgender former inmates reporting sexual abuse.[18]

"When I was in the joint," Frazier continues, "rape wasn't just something you could let happen to you," and then proceeds to engage in some heavy victim-blaming: "From what I witnessed, it was quite common for a transgender inmate to get 'married' behind bars" to a "big, dreaded prison dude known as 'Bubba.'"

And just in case we weren't clear on the fact that Frazier is now actively fantasizing about Manning being raped in prison—and remember, *The Daily Beast* enthusiastically published this column—Frazier leaves us on a sunny note: "We need to keep in mind that one person's prison is another person's palace. Chelsea Manning could become the queen bee."

These examples of shocking ignorance on the part of our media highlight why the fight for equality doesn't end with a wedding. Until there is overarching federal protection for LGBT individuals, the truth is that their rights as human beings still fall to the whims of elections, and are subject to referendums on a state-by-state basis.

Imagine a world in which "Proposition 12: Redheads shouldn't be allowed to marry" existed on a ballot. Sure, you may not like redheads. Maybe they creep you out a little bit. Maybe you've even constructed an emergency bunker stocked with canned foods and axes just in case there's a redhead uprising. Maybe you don't understand how they live fulfilling lives unable to go to the beach (side note: WE MANAGE JUST FINE, thank you), but that doesn't mean we, as a society, should punish people for the way they're born.

Citizens are only as informed as their media is informative. You, dear reader, can't learn about the baseless fear-mongering behind a Proposition 12 unless your media clearly presents the facts. Instead, the media brings on Pundit A to speak on behalf of redheads, and then Pundit B to tell wild tales about how redheads feed on human souls.

Expanding human rights has never once led to the downfall of our society. If anything, it has strengthened our culture—making it more diverse and empowering for individuals. Whether we're talking about the civil rights movement, or women's suffrage, or LGBT rights, time and time again, the media has clung to outdated notions, and it's only when the popular will becomes undeniable that it changes its tune.

One day, young people will look back and laugh at the notion that anyone thought same-sex marriage would lead to bestiality or that repealing DADT would result in the collapse of the military, and they'll wonder why that silly man with the white beard on CNN kept interviewing evangelical radicals who shouted about gays burning in hell for all eternity.

And you'll be able to say, "Once there was this thing called the mainstream media, and it was a terrible thing, Susie. There was constant shouting, and flashing graphics, and no one could learn a thing . . ."

CHAPTER 6

Fuck the NRA: Guns Don't Kill People; People with Dangerously Underfunded Mental Health Care Programs Do (with Guns)

It's difficult to keep this chapter up-to-date because every time the authors revise the text to include the latest horrific mass shooting, another gun-related tragedy unfolds somewhere in America.

On December 14, 2012, a young man named Adam Lanza fatally shot twenty children and six adult staff members at Sandy Hook Elementary School in the small community of Sandy Hook, a village in Newtown, Connecticut. Before the massacre, Lanza killed his mother in their home, and after the elementary school shooting, Lanza took his own life.

In total, twenty-eight people died.

More recently, on September 16, 2013, Aaron Alexis, a lone gunman, fatally shot twelve people and injured three others in a mass shooting at the headquarters of the Naval Sea Systems Command inside the Washington Navy Yard. Thirteen people died, including Alexis, who was killed by police.

This was the second-deadliest mass murder on a US military

base after the 2009 Fort Hood shooting in which thirteen people were killed and more than thirty injured.

In the same way that Americans were collectively horrified after the Columbine massacre, and the Virginia Tech shooting, and the Sikh temple shooting (okay, maybe a lot of racist Americans overlooked that one), and the Aurora theater shooting, and the slew of shootings in Chicago (again, maybe we don't pay as much attention to that because poor black kids are the victims there), people were once again shocked—shocked!—that this kind of gun violence could happen in a sleepy community like Sandy Hook or in an ostensibly secure location like the Washington Navy Yard.

Of course, by saying, "this kind of thing doesn't happen here," there's an implication that horrific gun violence is *supposed* to happen in certain *other* places, say, Chicago's South Side, but not in, say, the white-dominated northeastern community of Sandy Hook.

But we digress.

All of these recent mass shootings are tragedies and none is more or less tragic than the others, but when the victims are a classroom full of defenseless children and their teachers, it does lend a few more decibels to the national outcry, and at the time, it seemed that Sandy Hook would reignite a debate long ago surrendered by moderate Democrats: massacre prevention. Because that's what we're really talking about. No longer is it entirely accurate to call the quest for gun regulation "gun control" because in the wake of twenty children being penned in their classroom and exterminated by a mentally disturbed young man, what we really need to start talking about is stopping massacres from happening, and one of the ways we can hope to reach that goal is through gun regulation.

Now, this is usually where your conservative uncle who has

a concealed carry permit for all those pesky gangland scenarios in his gated community down in Lauderdale says, "But what if I had a knife? I could still kill people then! What if I had a screwdriver?? I could drive it into my neighbor's stupid head!" And that's when you should tell your uncle he should not be allowed to have sharp objects and maybe should invest in an anger management seminar. Also, of course you can kill people with other objects aside from guns, but the point is it's a lot more difficult to commit *massacres* with objects that aren't guns. In fact, the same day as the Sandy Hook shooting, a man in China went on a stabbing spree in a school. People were indeed hurt, but not a single person died.

The Constitution was written a long time ago—back when the founders were imagining militias armed with muskets—and if the theater shooting in Colorado had gone down with a musket, James Holmes would have been tackled after his first shot when he paused to jam a pipe into the barrel to reload, and then probably beaten with his own musket.

Given the tone we have set for this chapter, it may surprise you that at least one of the authors doesn't harbor irrational hatred of guns or gun owners.

Allison grew up thinking guns were part of working people's daily lives. Most of her extended family are police officers, so she was accustomed to associating guns with protection—sort of a default accessory of the good guys.

One summer, while vacationing with her family in upstate New York, she engaged in a target contest with her cousin, who used a BB rifle. Again, seeing a rifle didn't faze Allison because hunters carry rifles, and only deer should fear hunters.

Not being a deer, she wasn't afraid, and even tried her hand at shooting the rifle a few times, and then decided to really challenge herself with the bow.

As it turns out, an arrow does not have the same consistent accuracy as a rifle. Around the fifth time Allison missed the target entirely, her cousin nodded thoughtfully and remarked: "Well, I guess that's why the Indians lost."

Jamie, on the other hand, is a tiny scared person and was not raised around guns. If he had been, he would have spent his entire childhood fainting.

Gun Control Is Like "Man Abortion"

In 2013, right between the Sandy Hook and Washington Navy Yard shootings, Jamie had an encounter with a gun enthusiast. Picture it: He was on an airplane going through his usual routine of doing everything in his power to avoid having awkward conversations with strangers. He was wearing headphones, and just as an extra bit of precaution, reading a book. Headphones *and* a book. No matter which hemisphere of his body you looked at, the signs pointed to: Do Not Disturb.

Within thirty seconds, a young man wearing a beanie and a libertarian beard poked him and said, "Hey man, you like cars?" (*Editor's note: the thought of Jamie talking about cars is laughable to anyone who knows him.*)

Jamie politely said no, and without skipping a beat the bearded stranger said, "Cool! Check it out!" and busted out a car magazine. Jamie sighed. The kid seemed nice enough, so Jamie nodded along to a whole host of things he knew nothing about—occasionally trying to jump in with any story he could think of involving a car.

Bearded Libertarian: Check out the tires on this baby!

Jamie: One time I had a Saturn and drove it in New York but was too afraid to parallel park. It's made of plastic. CARS HAVE ENGINES!

Since the car conversation was going so swimmingly, Bearded Libertarian thought *why not talk about politics?* Now, usually when you talk about politics to a complete stranger on an airplane, you open soft and ease into the conversation.

Not this guy. Jamie's new friend decided to go with, "So what are your thoughts on guns?"

Holy shit. I better tread carefully, thought Jamie. *Gun control is like "man abortion." Guys with beards take that shit very seriously.*

Next, Bearded Libertarian starts listing all the guns he owns. Then he starts listing all the guns that he illegally owns. On a plane. *Loudly.* Post-9/11.

But no one said a thing! Probably because he was white. If anyone who even looked vaguely Arab, like a Mexican or a very tan Jew, started listing all the small arms they own, the pilot would have nose-dived the plane toward the ocean, while singing the "Star-Spangled Banner" over the intercom.

In fact, a week before this encounter, two unidentified men detonated a bomb in Boston, and shortly after, two Arab men were removed from a plane for being suspicious. Were they listing all the guns they owned? Nope! They were speaking Arabic! Their *language.* But somebody nearby was like "Hey! Those don't sound like Bruce Springsteen lyrics! Get 'em!"

What the first Arab guy was probably saying was, "That guy is looking at us strangely," and then the other guy said, "Shit." And then they were arrested. Oddly enough, they were found innocent and released.

Now, Jamie's new bearded buddy is just *one* gun fanatic. This isn't a peer-reviewed study conducted by a terrified Jamie riding airplane after airplane over the course of ten years, like a skinny Jewish George Clooney in *Up in the Air*, but we do know that in America today, fewer people own more guns. According to a 2012 CNN analysis of gun ownership data, a decreasing number of American gun owners own two-thirds of the nation's guns and as many as one-third of the guns on the planet.[1]

On the planet.

What this data would seem to suggest is that a small group of gun enthusiasts are stockpiling munitions. Why might that be? Well, we're pretty sure it's because many of them are paranoid, and in some cases, delusional. But they would probably tell you it's because the Mexicans are coming to take their jobs as Lynyrd Skynyrd impersonators.

Aaaaaanyway . . . Bearded Libertarian went on to ask Jamie (without lowering his voice) how he feels about conspiracies. What Jamie *should* have said was, "The same way I feel about this EMERGENCY EXIT!!!" and jumped to his death rather than further engage the crazy in seat 12A. But what he *did* say was, "Ehhhhhhh."

Bearded Libertarian saw this as Jamie's way of saying, "Please tell me about that video you just watched on YouTube called 'Osama Is Obama.'" Which he did, and then spent thirty minutes trying to convince Jamie that Barack Obama, the president of the United States, is actually Osama bin Laden, a dead terrorist.

First of all, that's racist. Second, you can't just combine shit you don't like because you think all brown people look the same! That's lazy. You can hate Barack Obama, and also hate Osama bin Laden. You don't need to mash them together like some weird racist smorgasbord of hate. The authors don't run around town screaming, "THATCHER IS NICKELBACK!" We hate both of them. You can hate more than one thing simultaneously.

Third, the man who thinks the president is a terrorist is armed to the fucking teeth with high-powered weapons.

Many gun enthusiasts claim they have the right to own vast quantities of munitions, including assault weapons that can, as in the case of Fort Hood, shoot twenty rounds in just 5.3 seconds, because it's "in the Constitution" and they need to "protect their families."

But the thing is, Americans *don't* need automatic weapons to protect themselves. In our lifetimes, there is a chance we will be mugged or burglarized, but we can say with certainty that none of us will have a rogue group of ex–Special Forces come crashing into our homes, whom we will need to take out with machine guns and bullets that pierce through protective gear. Unless you're Liam Neeson and you're reading this. And if you are Liam Neeson and you're reading this: AWESOME.

Also, in the cases of individuals who ARE planning some kind of take-on-the-military militia melee, maybe the US government shouldn't encourage that behavior by deregulating gun sales until the point where one individual can horde a huge cache of weapons to "go teach the black guy in the White House a lesson."

As for hunting, we're pretty positive that deer don't have bullet-proof vests. A regular gun, i.e., a rifle, will suffice when killing an animal that can barely handle crossing the street. (Unless you're a hunter who's that much of a coward that you need a machine gun to murder an animal that can in no way fight back and doesn't have thumbs.)

You're Not Rambo and You
Shouldn't Dress Like Him Either

Forty percent of guns are sold at gun shows where background checks are not required by law. And even though the NRA loves to tout the figure that there are 300 million guns in the United States to give the illusion that every single American is armed, those guns are concentrated in fewer and fewer hands. The NRA wants you to believe that, nowadays, most freedom-loving Americans have a family gun that they go out and shoot together on Christmas Eve to honor the birth of the baby Jesus.

In reality, a lot of crazy people have a lot of guns. You know who needs more than one gun? People who are "preparing" for "bad shit" to "go down." So it's to be expected when a man like Von I. Meyer is arrested in Indiana shortly after the Sandy Hook massacre, armed with forty-seven guns after threatening to "kill as many people as he could" at an elementary school near his house. Fewer people own a majority of the nation's guns, and not all of them are firing on all cylinders.

On *Citizen Radio*, we have tried to reshape the conversation on gun control, and steer it away from perceptions of weakness and capitulation toward what we call massacre prevention. After the tragic 2012 Newtown shooting, *Citizen Radio* attempted to frame the dialogue as a way to avoid the future deaths of innocent children. Though the mood recording that day was subdued (considering twenty-eight human beings had just died), we also relentlessly mocked politicians and pundits who in the aftermath of the New-town massacre crafted genius policy suggestions such as arming teachers and installing metal detectors in elementary schools. The response we got from our listeners was surprising. People seemed amazed that we were willing to honor the victims, not by suggesting implementing police state tactics, but by remaining uncompromising in our position on gun control.

Progressive caveat: guns cannot be blamed for all of the country's ills. For example, the fact that the US government has enthusiastically worked to defund mental health care programs is also a leading cause of mentally ill people going undiagnosed and unsupervised. Combine a lackluster social safety net with underregulated gun markets, and you have a perfect storm of senseless death.

So what happens when the zombie apocalypse arrives, or the government wants to destroy America, or any other online fantasy written by Reddit user GUNZ4367 comes true? Well, either nothing, or the Oklahoma City bombing. People who talk about stockpiling arms for the end-of-the-world-type situations are either lonely Jason Statham wannabes, or people who want the end of the world to happen so badly they plan on initiating it, and those people need help and therapy—not a shitload of weaponry.

We at *Citizen Radio* hear this all the time: "You criticize the government so much, and you're telling me you want them to have all the guns?!"

First of all, we don't harbor fantasies of assassinating people who work in the government. Sure, maybe we've posted pictures of Mitch McConnell tripping over his own shoelaces a lot, but that's about as far as that goes.

Second, let's say the government does decide to strike and

obliterate all dissidents. Let's say Michelle Obama enacts a chocolate ban and there's an uprising and it's every man and woman for themselves. America has a government, and by extension a military, that is in the business of, on a fairly regular basis, destroying entire Middle Eastern countries.

You think your stockpile of weapons, impressive as it may be for a regular Joe, has any prayer of taking on the US military? You going to get all *Red Dawn* up in here? You? Tom from North Dakota? ARE YOU THE HERO WE'VE BEEN WAITING FOR?! Your gun may be able to mow down a bunch of elementary school kids, but it can't stop a tank.

Even though not a single massacre has been stopped by a *Halo 3* player who happened to be walking by the scene of the crime, armed with his own personal AK-47 and draped with ammunition à la Sylvester Stallone in *Rambo*, many people still cling to this fantasy. Now, some of these people are violent idiots, but some of them also mean well. A lot of times, when one first hears about a tragedy like Newtown, it's easy to slip into denial.

Sure, you're sad, but you're also angry and you start to picture a world where it never happened. How could this have been stopped? And some people, in order to cope with a deluge of emotions, start getting mad at everyone, including themselves. *Well, if I had been there, I would have stopped it,* they think. *Why didn't someone just shoot this motherfucker?! Why didn't the children have tiny rifles?!*

In *The Daily Beast*, Megan McArdle proposed a rather unorthodox solution to future Newtown-like massacres when she recommended that children gang-rush crazed gunmen in order to take out their attackers:

If we drilled it into young people that the correct thing to do is for everyone to instantly run at the guy with the gun, these sorts of mass shootings would be less deadly, because even a guy with a very powerful weapon can be brought down by 8–12 unarmed bodies piling on him at once. Would it work? Would people do it? I have no idea; all I can say is that both these things would be more effective than banning rifles with pistol grips.[2]

Sure, children could do that, or we could, ya know, make sure dangerous people can't get their hands on sophisticated weaponry. It's really unfair that the burden of massacre prevention is heaped upon the potential future victims of such tragedies. Innocent children are expected to learn in an environment where there are metal detectors, random locker searches, bomb-sniffing dogs, and now they're expected to take out the gunman too?

While we're at it, you know what else won't stop school shootings? Like, at all? Special Agent Math Teacher. And the same people calling for that "solution" are also the same folks who don't trust teachers to unionize, but suddenly they trust them enough to teach their children whilst packing heat. Maybe all of those hero teachers (who, remember, already get paid too much, according to the people who want them to add target practice to their workday) wouldn't have saved all those other children at Sandy Hook if they were busy trying to lock and load.

Being a teacher is hard and time-consuming enough! The teachers we know work fourteen-hour days, most of it off the clock, buy their kids treats, stickers, and supplies with their own money, then turn on Fox News and hear some millionaire, whose only job is to take money from his rich parents, talking about how we pay for teachers' luxurious lives and how they are selfish. We don't know how many posh teacher dinner parties these pundits have been to, but we imagine the guest list is pretty limited, considering it's hard to have them inside studio apartments. (And sure, some teachers make more than others, blah, blah, blah, this is the NRA chapter, not the education chapter! Let us make our point!)

Teachers don't even get paid enough to be teachers, let alone police-officer-teachers. Also, did you see the kind of stress this idea put on poor Arnold Schwarzenegger in *Kindergarten Cop*? He had like three panic attacks, and that was only a 111-minute movie.

More importantly, you cannot learn how to be an accurate shot by taking a couple firearm workshops. Hell, trained cops can't even do it half the time. Remember the shoot-out by the Empire State Building in 2012 when cops shot nine civilians? These are officers who are trained ALL THE TIME how to use their weapons. They had to pass tests! Tests with guns!

You know what wouldn't have made the Sandy Hook incident better? Crossfire. More armed people, shooting wildly into a chaotic situation is never, ever, ever a good idea.

. . . Nor Are You Bruce Willis, or Channing Tatum, or Jamie Foxx

When Gabrielle Giffords was shot, the only armed civilian there almost opened fire on another innocent civilian, and in the Colorado movie theater, there was a shooter standing in a crowded, dark, smoke-filled room where crossfire would have landed more people in the hospital. Adding more guns to the massacres wouldn't have helped.

And in case you doubt that reasoning, the state of Florida helpfully supplied some supporting evidence in January 2014 when retired police officer Curtis Reeves was sitting in a movie theater, and the NRA will be delighted to learn that this upstanding member of Floridian society was armed. Hooray! Here is a gun enthusiast's ideal situation: a responsible man, exercising his Second Amendment rights in a movie theater, so if violence breaks out, Reeves would have been there to put a stop to it.

Of course, that's not what happened. Instead, Reeves got into an argument with a man who was texting, and then Reeves shot Chad Oulson in the chest and Oulson's wife, Nicole, in the hand. Chad Oulson died later at a hospital.[3]

The answer is not to add more guns.

After Virginia Tech, there was a right-wing cry to ARM THE STUDENTS! Since when does anyone think college students should moonlight as precision snipers? We don't trust these kids to play beer pong the right way, let alone take down armed assailants. You really want to give a gun to some shaky college freshman during exam week? He's already freaking out because he pulled two all-nighters in a row, his lab partner disappeared for some reason, and he's about to OD on Red Bull.

Oh, and in case you forgot—Columbine had an armed guard on campus, Virginia Tech had a police department, and Fort Hood is a fucking military base! The problem has never been that we don't have enough guns in these places. It's that dangerous people manage to get their hands on them.

How the Media Plays in to the "Guns as Self-Defense" Myth, and Steers the Conversation Away from Mental Health

Most school shootings are prevented—not stopped by armed teachers or guards or charging first graders—but *prevented* by information that keeps the massacre from ever happening to begin with. Massacres aren't stopped by everyone holding everyone else at gunpoint, but by students paying attention, looking for warning signs, and telling an adult if they think one of their fellow students is troubled.

Yet the media plays into the guns-equal-self-defense delusion.

Early in 2013, *This Week* host George Stephanopoulos failed to challenge former Republican senator Rick Santorum when he claimed, "There are more people who protect themselves and stop violence . . . happen[ing] to them with the ownership of a gun than [there are] people who commit crimes with a gun."[4]

Fox News also jumped on the Guns = Protection bandwagon. Sean Hannity's January 18, 2013, show featured NRA CEO Wayne LaPierre, who stated that the vast majority of the American public "deeply believes in the Second Amendment, deeply believes they have a right to protect themselves," followed by former congressman Asa Hutchinson, director of the NRA's National School Shield Project, who told Hannity that the solution to school shootings is "to have the armed, trained presence there to really protect the children."[5]

(At one point, the *National Review Online* said the Newtown massacre could have been stopped if only there had been more men around. Well, you know what? There WAS a man there, and he shot everybody.[6])

Discussing gun regulations on CBS's *Face the Nation*, anchor

Bob Schieffer endorsed the view that protection was a legitimate rationale for gun ownership: "By now, the pros and cons of the gun issue are well known. . . . Of course, there are legitimate reasons for both pleasure and protection to own guns."[7]

On January 9, 2013, CNN's Anderson Cooper hosted a segment that gave, according to the media watchdog group Fairness & Accuracy in Reporting, more or less equal weight to arguments for and against the notion that guns make us safer, concluding that it's hard to say for sure:

> The one true thing that we know about the gun debate here at home, that neither side has a monopoly on the truth, or even the facts, because the facts can be so hard to establish. One side has studies linking gun ownership with violent death. But correlation is not causation.

The other side has research showing when people are allowed to carry concealed weapons, violent crimes slow down. Yet newer studies cast doubt on that conclusion.[8]

And yet, as FAIR notes, it's really *not* that hard to study the effects of guns on public health and safety.

A favorite study of gun advocates, 1995's "Armed Resistance to Crime: The Prevalence and Nature of Self-Defense with a Gun" by Gary Kleck and Marc Gertz, and the 1998 book by researcher John Lott called *More Guns, Less Crime*, have both been convincingly challenged by the scientific community.

In case gun enthusiasts citing studies published nearly two decades ago isn't a bright enough warning flare, along came a 2004 meta-study of gun research published by the National Research Council of the National Academies of Science that found Lott's claims were not supported by his data. Meanwhile, the Harvard School of Public Health's David Hemenway took on Kleck and Gertz in "Survey Research and Self-Defense Gun Use: An Explanation of Extreme Overestimates," demonstrating that because of the nature of the data, Kleck and Gertz's self-reported phone survey finding 2.5 million defensive uses of guns per year was wildly exaggerated.[9]

For example, FAIR notes, Kleck and Gertz says guns were used to defend against 845,000 burglaries in 1992, a year in which the National Crime Victimization Survey says there were fewer than 6 million burglaries.

Hemenway, using facts from NCVS, concluded that someone was known to be home in just 22 percent of burglaries (1.3 million people), and that fewer than half of US households have firearms, and pointed out that therefore Kleck and Gertz ask us "to believe that burglary victims in gun-owning households use their guns in self-defense more than 100 percent of the time."

Hemenway also notes that respondents may not really understand the definition of "self-defense," meaning some individuals may think they're legally defending themselves when they draw a gun during a minor altercation.

NCVS, controlling for many of the problems in Kleck and Gertz's study, supported Hemenway's findings, reporting 65,000 defensive gun uses per year in their 1997 report. As of 2013, NCVS estimates are in the 100,000 range.

FAIR considered the fact that there are 300 million firearms in the United States, and roughly 80 million gun owners, and then compared the self-defense numbers to the gun crime numbers.

The National Institute of Justice reported in 2005, "11,346 persons were killed by firearm violence and 477,040 persons were victims of a crime committed with a firearm."

The NRA also wildly inflates the self-defense figure, claiming firearms are used over 2 million times a year for personal protection, but a 2013 paper from the Violence Policy Center states that during the period 2007–11 an annual average of 67,740 individuals used guns for self-defense. (And as mentioned previously, the definition of "self-defense" is very vague. See: George Zimmerman and Trayvon Martin.)[10]

Basically, the number of people who use guns to successfully defend themselves has been wildly overestimated; people use guns when other means of de-escalation are available, and quite often, they end up dying when they try to use guns as a mode of self-defense.

Preventing another Newtown is going to take an effort on multiple fronts, not just on the issue of gun control, but also properly funding mental health care programs and alleviating stress inducers like poverty and unemployment.

And it's going to take better media because ours has already grown bored of the Newtown massacre and the issue of gun control. The establishment media has a rich tradition of failing to stick with stories that require long-term coverage, mostly because networks don't want to fall behind in the ratings. Once stories segue from the flashy drama of children being murdered into the nitty-gritty policy aspects of preventing that from ever happening again, the major networks peace out and move on to the next story to guarantee them lots of viewers.

As political science professor Danny Hayes explains on the *Washington Post*'s Wonkblog:

Gun control coverage was profuse in the days and weeks after the shooting. With Democratic political leaders declaring that "we can't tolerate this anymore" and that "we are not doing enough to protect our citizens," the debate over guns took center stage. This is a frequent pattern after mass shootings, as the media's intense interest in such a dramatic event leads to a spike in coverage.

But, as typically happens, the media's attention eventually waned after the "issue attention cycle." After several weeks of a deluge of coverage—fueled in part by the president's issuing of 23 gun-related executive actions—journalists turned to newer stories, including the fiscal cliff and the ongoing budget debates. Gun control returned to the headlines in April, when a Senate bill that would have expanded background checks generated a flurry of coverage. But the story essentially died once the legislation did.[11]

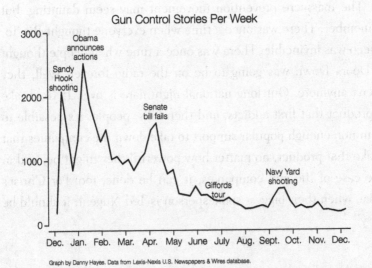

Gun Control Stories Per Week

Graph by Danny Hayes. Data from Lexis-Nexis U.S. Newspapers & Wires database.

The media getting distracted by a shiny object—the prospect of Democrats and Republicans bickering over the budget—is #newsfail.

It's up to the media to stick with these stories over the long term, and to stop pretending that researchers haven't extensively studied gun violence, and pretending we don't know guns do more harm than good. And meanwhile, you, gentle reader, can join your hosts at *Citizen Radio* in occupying the NRA: tell your representatives that they represent the people, not some good old boy organization whose members arm themselves because they still think the slave revolt might happen. Educate your friends laboring under the belief that guns provide safety. If you're an NRA member (first of all, congratulations on making it this far into this chapter), contact the NRA and say you don't agree with Wayne LaPierre's vision of an America where there are armed guards in every elementary school in the country.

The massacre prevention movement may seem daunting, but remember: There was once a time when everyone thought Big Tobacco was invincible. There was once a time when people thought 3 Doors Down was going to be on the radio forever. Well, they aren't anymore. Our long national nightmare is over. If you make a product that first addicts, and then kills, people, it's possible to summon enough popular support to take down the companies that make that product, no matter how powerful they might be, and in the case of the gun companies, it can be done, too. For Christ's sake, when their biggest spokesperson is Ted Nugent, it should be easy!

CHAPTER 7

We Know You Smoked Weed in College, Asshole:
How the War on Drugs Is Destroying This Country

In the United States, there is an assumption among some well-to-do individuals that prisons exist solely to house a certain demographic of undesirables, namely poor people and/or people of color. And because that assumption exists, popular opinion of recreational drug use has taken on a weird duality in which poor people who smoke crack are considered gross and dangerous and should definitely be incarcerated whereas little George Bushington III's cocaine-fueled freshman orientation at Harvard is considered harmless, youthful fun—a rite of passage, even—something every blue-blooded American boy is entitled to.

Which is why the disparity between minimum sentences for crack (a drug traditionally used by poor people of color) and powder cocaine (drug of choice for the generally white and wealthy) is eighteen to one. (The sentencing differential used to be one hundred to one until people were all, *Whaaaat, racist much?* and Congress agreed and passed the "Fair"[quotation marks ours] Sentencing Act in August 2010.) So even in "victory" (quotation marks ours), crack, or "black-people cocaine," still holds eighteen times the sentencing to its privileged cousin, regular old "white-frat-boy cocaine." (All quotation marks ours.)

Prepare to have your mind blown, gentle reader.

Cocaine and crack are virtually identical substances. It's true! Crack is just baking soda and water added to cocaine, and yet George Bushington III heads off to Wall Street, where he probably does even more purebred, fancy cocaine while poor people like forty-two-year-old Landon Thompson from Richmond, Virginia, are sentenced to life without parole for selling small amounts of crack cocaine.

"I think a life sentence for what you have done in this case is ridiculous," said federal district court judge James R. Spencer, the sentencing judge, who was forced in 2009 to give Thompson life in prison because of mandatory sentencing laws.

To give you an idea of how very big this problem is, the ACLU reports that about 79 percent of the 3,278 prisoners serving life without parole for nonviolent drug crimes have been sentenced to die in prison for violations similar to Thompson's.[1] Seventy-nine percent! That's like being stoned to death for jaywalking.

Or in other words: "Two niggers, two chinks, two greasers, or I don't stop the car. Why bother?" These words were spoken by a member of the Bath Township Police Department in Michigan and relayed to *Citizen Radio* by Howard Wooldridge, an ex-cop and veteran of the War on Drugs. Wooldridge served eighteen years in Bath Township, but retired in 1994, frustrated by what he says was too much law enforcement diverted to wasteful marijuana busts, primarily on people of color.

"I believe my profession is no more or less prejudiced than others," Wooldridge told us. "However, we have a badge, a gun, and arrest powers. The War on Drugs gives the racists an easy hook to hurt people they don't like. And they do."

Now, of course we believe that violent offenders of all races and ethnicities (drugged up or otherwise) should be punished. The authors do not equate smoking a small amount of recreational drugs with robbing a liquor store at gunpoint while high on methamphetamine. But our legal system *does* often equate seemingly disparate offenses in sentencing, at least where poor and minority populations are concerned. You *can* be locked up for the rest of your life for possessing a very small quantity of drugs (one prisoner serving a life sentence mentioned in the ACLU report was convicted for serving as a middleman in the sale of twenty dollars' worth of crack to an undercover officer), and the people most likely to get those sentences are poor minorities. This is a fact—it's not just something we commie pinkos at *Citizen Radio* make up to amuse ourselves.

And when you consider the fact that nationwide, one in three black men can expect to serve time behind bars, and that our prison population quintupled in a thirty-year period, it's clear that racial minorities have been targeted by the legal system. More African American men are in prison or jail, on probation or parole than were enslaved in 1850, before the Civil War began, according to Michelle Alexander, author of *The New Jim Crow: Mass Incarceration in the Age of Colorblindness*.[2] Blacks are incarcerated for drug offenses at much higher rates: even though only 13.5 percent of all drug *users* in the United States are black, 81 percent of federal drug *offenders* are black, with African Americans serving an average of six years for drug offenses, while whites are serving only four.[3] Another troubling statistic: many more black males have been incarcerated under drug prohibition in the United States than were jailed in South Africa during apartheid.

What's weird is: *locking people up doesn't stem drug use.* We know this because the biggest lock 'em up program of all, the War on Drugs, has been a spectacular failure. Even though law enforcement and the federal government threw a trillion dollars at the problem and imprisoned more people than any other country on the face of the earth, drugs have not magically disappeared from the American landscape.

A 2013 study published in the *British Medical Journal's BMJ Open* found that the prices of illegal drugs have generally declined, while their purity has increased over the past twenty years, raising serious doubts about the effectiveness of international law enforcement efforts to reduce drug supplies. We actually now have access to cheaper, stronger drugs, which we're pretty sure was not Dick Nixon's original intention.

You can't defeat "drugs" any more than you can defeat terrorism, or any other ideology or emotion. People take drugs to escape their shitty circumstances, the same way they binge-drink, or gamble, or engage in other scurrilous behaviors. In other words, people will stop taking drugs and/or selling drugs when they have opportunities to be happy, and find jobs and purposes they find fulfilling in which they're treated with dignity and as valued members of society. Oddly enough, having your family members rotting in prison for the rest of their lives over a twenty bag of crack does not help boost community spirit.

Let's take a trip down a road that anyone who watched *The Wire* is familiar with: children tend to emulate the behavior of their elders, right? And say your dad—or uncle, or older brother—is a dealer on your corner and has protected you since you were learning how to ride a bike. So you look up to him, and then one day he's locked up on a drug charge, and guess what happens next?

You start dealing in order to feed your family and provide protection for the kids younger than you. It's not so hard to imagine this scenario playing out over and over again in poor communities, is it? As opposed to a scenario in which all poor children are born evil and with completely equal opportunities to be raised into prosperity and Ivy League degrees but they *choose* to sling crack instead. But if you turn on the news, these kids are presented as hooligans plotting to destroy our society, rather than as the ones society left behind.

And so the authors ask you: what's more likely—completely wiping out illegal drugs in this country, or refining the system so that the poorest members of our society don't get hit with the harshest punishments for using or selling those drugs, which only results in the continuing cycle of poverty and degradation outlined above?

Furthermore, there appears to be no plan to reduce or cap the prison population. Especially now that more and more prisons—owned by big companies like CCA, GEO Group, and the Management & Training Corporation in states such as Tennessee, Florida, and Utah—are being privatized, lots of money can be made off of locking up citizens convicted of nonviolent crimes for extended periods of time, who have few people lobbying on their behalf.

Go Directly to Jail. Do Not Collect $200.
Especially If You Are a Minority

Now, you might be thinking, "But authors! I must ask you after reviewing these numbers: don't you think these young black people are bringing it on themselves?"

First, we'd like to say: Hello, Donald Trump! Thanks so much for buying our book!

Second, a LOT of people of all ethnicities do drugs, it's true. Whether it's Rush "Morals" Limbaugh with his happy pills, Ted Haggard with his (alleged) meth-induced denial romps, or countless white suburban brats across the country, MANY white people ingest all kinds of drugs (legal and illegal) in order to escape reality or manage pain. However, African American communities are *targeted* more aggressively. Meaning: more police resources are devoted to harassing poor communities of color, and as a result, people of color are incarcerated at high rates. All kinds of racial profiling programs arose out of the War on Drugs, including proxy programs like Stop and Frisk in New York City, which the department claims stops violent crime and drug sales. According to the ACLU, police have stopped more than 4 million New Yorkers since 2002, and blacks and Latinos continue to be the overwhelming targets of these tactics. However, nearly nine out of ten people stopped-and-frisked have been completely innocent—this is according to the NYPD's own reports—meaning the individuals stopped were not in fact in possession of a weapon or drugs.[4]

There are countless kids in jail for possession of weed when the worst thing they've ever done while high was misquote *The Simpsons*. On the other hand, we're all familiar with the horrific consequences of alcohol abuse. For example: alcohol poisoning, DUIs, addiction, running the country for eight years and starting several illegal wars, most country music, et cetera.

Alcohol kills more people than crack, cocaine, and heroin combined. That's insane! Not only is it legal, but it is promoted! Like, all the time! You're never going to see a commercial during the Super Bowl halftime with several naked girls climbing all over some nerdy guy with a voice-over saying, "You want to be the life of the party? Well, then it's CRACK TIME!"

But with alcohol, profits go to giant corporations instead of street dealers, so it's considered an acceptable American industry run by upright citizens such as Peter Swinburn (CEO, Molson Coors, white guy), Tom Long (CEO, MillerCoors, white guy), Martin F. Roper (CEO, Boston Beer Company, white guy), and the list goes on.

Funny how the War on Drugs has never once been construed as a war on the most damaging and insidious drug of all.

The Drunk Firefighter Is Not Here to Help: A Parable

When the authors were struggling to make a living eight years ago, we got ourselves a car, and decided to drive around the country collecting stories, writing, and performing. Did we do this because someone gave us a copy of *On the Road*, and we were extremely high and impressionable, you ask?

Shut up.

We went to see our parents to tell them we loved them (read: beg for money) before we left town, and as we were pulling away from our farewells, our car was rear-ended. Like, smashed. See, we drove a Saturn, which is made of plastic and wishes, so it was literally turned into an accordion.

Horrified and shaking, we got out to see a drunk man in a firefighter's uniform standing next to our car, swaying slightly.

"Oh, s'not bad," he slurred, staring glassy-eyed at our destroyed vehicle.

But, lo! The heavens did smile upon us at that moment

because there just so happened to be a police officer parked across the street for the purposes of writing a young lady a speeding ticket and/or flirting with a young lady who was charming her way out of a speeding ticket.

"Come, good sir!" we shouted. "Save us from this wretch!"

And that's when the law officer held up his finger (the universal sign of "One minute, you idiots") as the drunk firefighter proceeded to backstep, climb back into his truck, and make THE SLOWEST GETAWAY IN THE HISTORY OF THE WORLD.

Of course, neither of the authors had thought to get the license plate number because at the time we were still full of hope and love and belief that police officers are competent members of our society.

We had no money to pay for the damage done to the car, so Jamie decided to nail the culprit himself by going to every firehouse in the area, searching for the hit-and-runner. When he arrived at the first firehouse, the chief listened to his story and replied: "NOOoooo! Oh God, NO! JIMMY! Oh, poor, poor Jimmy. He did it again. I can't believe it! No! NO! NOOO! Let me grab a picture of him so you can ID him, but I KNOW! I know it's him . . ."

He showed Jamie the photo. Jimmy was not the drunk driver.

Fifteen minutes later, Jamie arrived at a second firehouse: "FRANK! NO! NOOOOOOO! Sweet prince, Frank! OFF THE WAGON! Damn you, Frank! DAMN YOU TO HELL!"

It wasn't Frank, either.

This happened six times. No joke. Six. Every firehouse had one known DUI guy, and none of them was the guy that smashed our crappy car.

Even cops and firefighters love booze. We tax booze. Booze is an important part of our economy, and (often right-wing) billionaires like the Coors family make millions keeping it flowing for the Jimmys and Franks of the world.

Legalization: It's Not Just Your Stoner Friend Steve's Idea Anymore

Since the War on Drugs is an obvious failure and waste of taxpayer cash, you'd think politicians—the men and women elected by THE PEOPLE—would feel pressured to do away with this whole system and start fresh. Maybe even by legalizing and regulating some of those nonalcoholic drugs to bring in billions of dollars in tax revenue, curb the dangerous black market drug trade, and free up cops to chase down real criminals.

But politicians don't want to look soft on crime. Crafting a platform of empathy and prisoner rehabilitation has historically, at least in the United States, been a great way to get on the fast track to political exile. Basically, due to a fear of looking *weak* and *soft* and *French*, political leaders run to the opposite end of the spectrum of human constitution and land somewhere around "completely fascist."

Here is an example of a political attack ad that might run against a politician who publicly states that the War on Drugs is a failure. Please read in a very scary voice:

Senator Riley thinks the War on Drugs is failing. I wonder if Senator Riley came up with this notion while BLOWING POT SMOKE IN YOUR BABY'S FACE! Oh, you don't know where your baby is right now? Well, in Senator Riley's world, he has been sold into baby prostitution, so his baby pimp can buy baby crack. DO YOU WANT TO LIVE IN A WORLD WITH BABY WHORES?! Senator Riley does.

[Fade out on a picture of the senator talking to black people.]

In 2000, former president Bill Clinton sat down for an interview with *Rolling Stone* and casually stated he believes small amounts of marijuana should be decriminalized.[5]

Hmm . . . If only he had been in a position of enormous power for EIGHT FUCKING YEARS to make that happen. See, a funny thing happens when Democratic presidents leave the White House and become civilians again: they turn into raging liberals. It's as if they magically transform into the hard-core lefties that liberals THOUGHT they were voting for in the first place as soon as they clear the White House lawn. It's like when you see your asshole chemistry teacher after hours at a bar, and are like, wait, you're a normal person?

While they still hold the reins of power, presidents tend instead to treat the issue of decriminalization as an unserious question posed by unhinged stoners.

President Obama participated in a 2009 online town hall in which 13,728 questions were submitted to the president, and the top six questions in the popular "Budget" category, as well as top questions in the "Health Care Reform" and "Green Jobs" categories addressed pot and drug legalization.

Here was the president's response:

Three point five million people voted. I have to say that there was one question that was voted on that ranked fairly high and that was whether legalizing marijuana would improve the economy [*laughter*] and job creation. And I don't know what this says about the online audience [*laughter*] but I just want—I don't want people to think that—this was a fairly popular question; we want to make sure that it was answered. The answer is, no, I don't think that is a good strategy [*laughter*] to grow our economy. [*Applause*]⁶

Sarcastic clapping from the authors.

See, it's FUNNY that millions of people are in jail for nonviolent drug offenses, tearing apart families and communities, and it's FUNNY that we're burning $16.9 billion per year incarcerating them, and it's FUNNY the nation has 5 percent of the world's population yet 25 percent of its prisoners, and 500,000 people are currently locked up for nonviolent drug offenses, and it's downright HILARIOUS that our prisons have become warehouses for society's "undesirables," and now this system is being privatized to reap vast fortunes on behalf of companies for the accomplishment of jailing human beings.

It's like Obama thinks the internet is this mythical land where only hippies wander around stoned, bumping into things while looking for vegan brownies to satisfy their munchies. In Obama's world, the internet = Portland.

And yet, respected medical and legal professionals in other parts of the world (i.e., not Portland) have demonstrated that there are alternatives to waging a never-ending War on Drugs.

Take, for example, Gabor Maté, a Canadian physician who specializes in the study and treatment of addiction, and works with addicts at North America's only supervised injection site (a place where addicts can go to legally shoot up their illegal drugs in a safe environment and not be subjected to arrest). Maté works on Insite's detox floor, where addicts detox for up to two weeks before moving up to the third floor of the building, where they await housing or placement in rehabilitation programs. (While staying in the Insite detox ward, they cannot use drugs.)

In an interview with *Citizen Radio*, Maté said the purpose of Insite is to reduce harm from injection.

"We're not providing the drugs. . . . But we are providing a place where under legal exemption, people can inject without being arrested, and staff can help them without being arrested. Many studies have shown that as a result, there's less disease transmission because obviously people are not using dirty needles and not sharing needles. So hepatitis C and HIV, which are the scourges of the drug-using community, are kept at bay. People also develop fewer body infections, joint infections, there's less bacteria being introduced into their veins and so on. On that level, it's simply a harm-reduction facility, which more than justifies, both medically and economically, its existence."

But beyond the practical benefits of not spreading diseases and infections, Insite is also a place where addicts are treated as human beings instead of as criminals.

"It's the only place and the first place that many drug addicts, street-level drug addicts, have any kind of contact with compassionate health care," Maté said. "Don't forget, again, that these people's history is that of abuse and marginalization and they really live as outcasts on the social periphery. To have a facility where they get a cup of coffee and are treated kindly, that's a step forward for them and it's also, for some of them, a step forward toward recovery. So that the facility serves the purpose of reducing harm and of introducing people to a different model of care, which for many of them is completely new."

Furthermore, we have proof that decriminalization works! In 2009, Glenn Greenwald wrote a report for the Cato Institute about Portugal's efforts at drug decriminalization, and the data shows, judged by virtually every metric, that Portugal's framework is a resounding success.[7]

The most impressive finding is that Portugal hasn't regressed into a nation of drugged-out criminals. Following decriminalization, Portugal had the lowest rate of lifetime marijuana use in people over fifteen in the EU (10 percent). Meanwhile, in the United States the figure for marijuana users over twelve is 39.8 percent. More Americans have used cocaine than Portuguese have used marijuana.

Rates of lifetime use of any illegal drug among seventh through ninth graders fell; drug use in older teens also declined; lifetime heroin use among sixteen- to eighteen-year-olds fell, although there was a slight increase in marijuana use in that age group (but be real: would you rather have kids using heroin or weed?).

New HIV infections in drug users fell and deaths related to heroin and similar drugs were cut by more than half. Encouragingly, the number of people on methadone and buprenorphine treatment for drug addiction rose to 14,877 from 6,040 after decriminalization, and money saved on enforcement allowed for increases in drug-free treatment funding.

(Side note: Even Nixon recognized the importance of recovery and included generous funding for rehabilitation programs in the original budget for the War on Drugs. Unfortunately, Nixon ultimately failed to take his own advice, and oversaw the spending of hundreds of millions of dollars in order to militarize the US-Mexico border.)

In January 2014, Obama sat down for an interview with the

New Yorker's David Remnick in which the president said all the right things about pot and legalization. "As has been well documented, I smoked pot as a kid, and I view it as a bad habit and a vice, not very different from the cigarettes that I smoked as a young person up through a big chunk of my adult life," Obama said. "I don't think it is more dangerous than alcohol."

Well said, Mr. President! But don't you think the War on Drugs is also classist and racist?

"Middle-class kids don't get locked up for smoking pot, and poor kids do," he said. "And African American kids and Latino kids are more likely to be poor and less likely to have the resources and the support to avoid unduly harsh penalties."

Holy shit! This is amazing. But what about your colleagues (and yourself) and everyone involved in maintaining the War on Drugs who also admit to having smoked weed in the past? Doesn't that make you a bunch of hypocrites?

"We should not be locking up kids or individual users for long stretches of jail time when some of the folks who are writing those laws have probably done the same thing," Obama added.[8]

Wow. What amazing, sparkling words (with which we totally agree!).

The only problem is that Obama's pretty words don't equal meaningful policy changes, and even though the president also gave his blessing to states like Colorado's efforts to legalize pot, his talk is still only that—talk.

Flashbacks of Bill Clinton in 2000. You're the president, dude! If you really wanted to enact change, use the bully pulpit. Don't just play the part of hip dad in magazine interviews.

Now, let's go over some of the things we've learned in this chapter: People of color are incarcerated at much higher rates, to fail at its inception because drug crime doesn't function like other kinds of crime. Cole explains:

> [W]hen officers arrested a robber or rapist, the number of rapes and robberies declines. . . . But when I arrested a drug dealer the number of drug sales didn't change at all. I was simply creating a job opening for a long line of people more than willing to risk arrest for those obscene profits. It was actually worse than that. I wasn't just creating a job opening; I was creating a safe job opening because if they tried to get the job while the dealer was still on the corner he would probably shoot them. I would suggest to you that whole armies of police cannot stop drug trafficking when the profits are this immense.[15]

As for many advocates for ending the War on Drugs, Legalize and Regulate is Cole's mantra. *But won't that cause everyone to use drugs?* you might ask him. Cole has a pretty simple response to that question. "Drugs were not illegal in this country until 1914 and we seemed to get through the first 200 years without that occurring."

Ding!

Just Let Grandma Get High

Aside from the people who enjoy getting high for the sake of getting high, and the people dealing drugs in order to make a living and support their families, there is a third group—sick patients— who need access to illegal drugs in order to ease their pain.

It's difficult to know how many people use medicinal marijuana because the records are sketchy. For example, California does not require residents to register as patients, and of the twenty states (plus the District of Columbia) that allow the medicinal use of cannabis, it is one of only three without such a requirement. California NORML estimates that 1.1 million people are licensed for medical marijuana in that state alone.

But we know there are grandmas like seventy-year-old Betty (not her real name), who told New Jersey's PIX 11 that she has resorted to treating her rare form of liver cancer by buying street pot. She tried going for a marijuana prescription from New Jersey's pot dispensary, but the demand has outgrown supply in the state, and she was unable to legally buy and smoke marijuana.

"Without it, I'd be dead," Betty told PIX. "I couldn't eat, I was throwing up constantly. I lost forty-five pounds." But now able to smoke pot, she has an appetite again and is "healthy enough to have the tumor on her liver removed," the news outlet reports.[16]

Patients like Betty are now forced to stand on the front lines protesting for medicinal marijuana, instead of resting as they should, because the feds are busting into their dispensaries like they're looking for the Taliban.

On the other hand, alcohol—which has its own "dispensaries" called bars, liquor stores, grocery stores, gas stations, et cetera—doesn't help sick people (unless you need to induce vomiting, or your ex-girlfriend who you swore you would never talk to again has the cure to your disease and only alcohol will give you the false courage to call her).

Most things can be done in moderation: drinking, getting high, medicating, eating dessert, you name it. Some people can do the moderation thing, some people can't. The authors can go out and have water all night while watching our friends drink, and wake up at six a.m. to work out. But if you put vegan cake in front of us . . . it's over.

The point is: everyone has their own vices, it is not the government's job to say some vices are okay and some will land individuals a lifetime in jail, especially considering how, oftentimes, the legal vices are more dangerous, more addictive, and easier to buy in bulk.

Of course, there do exist those who can't control their vices and these people are addicts who need help—but prison doesn't help addicts. It sucks them in and spits them back into a society where they are now considered even lesser citizens than when they first entered jail. Now, they may have lost the right to vote, access to public housing, and certain public assistance programs, all because they're sick, and in the United States, sick people are easier to lock up than to help.

Addicts won't get help by making license plates. They need counseling, detox clinics, access to clean needles, and rehab, just as cancer patients need reliable access to medicine that has proven effective and affordable. These demographics represent huge swaths of the drug-using population that could be aided by legalization and free up untold man-hours and budget dollars from law enforcement—not to mention beds in our already overcrowded prisons.

Imagine a world in which the United States would no longer have to arrest 1.9 million people every year for nonviolent drug offenses. And the savings wouldn't stop there. Since 1971, the United States has spent well over $1 trillion on an unwinnable war during a time when our infrastructure is crumbling, and public workers are having their pensions slashed. When the ruling elite claim there just "isn't enough to go around," the War on Drugs is consistently the first program offered up by citizens as an example of wasteful government spending that needs to be cut.

Many current and former law enforcement agents, such as the members of Law Enforcement Against Prohibition, believe the US government should import or produce the drugs and control them for quality, potency, and standardized measurement. Just as individuals died during alcohol prohibition by attempting to concoct "bathtub gin," so individuals now die by experimenting with the potency of drugs. If drugs were monitored by the FDA much as prescription pills are now monitored, overdoses would vastly decline. Then, once the drugs are made legal, the government can tax their sales. That would be one way out of this economic depression.

But can you picture Bill O'Reilly selling that line in prime time? He might have more luck with this:

Drug legalization isn't just a domestic security issue, it also has international implications. Terrorists "make a killing" off prohibition because of the basic principles of economics.

Check this out: In 1997, ten kilograms of reactor-grade plutonium (enough to make an atomic bomb) was valued at $56,000. The "average terrorist" makes his living selling illegal drugs. Heroin, which at the beginning of the War on Drugs in 1970 was valued at $400,000 per kilogram, is still worth $70,000 per kilogram today, despite the immense drop in price caused by the glut of supply created by thirty-seven years of a failed war on drugs. That means the "average terrorist" would have to sell about eight kilograms of pure heroin for every ten kilograms of pure weapons-grade plutonium he wishes to buy. That is not a major problem for the terrorist, as long as we continue the policy of drug prohibition.[17]

But if drug prohibition ended tomorrow, and the government

worked to regulate the drugs, terrorists couldn't sell heroin at the inflated market price. Basically, those "You're funding terrorism" antidrug commercials have inverted reality.

In actuality, it's the US government and its policy of drug prohibition that is aiding the terrorists.

Puff on that.

CHAPTER 8

USA! USA! USA! We're Here to Help . . .
with ~~Drones~~ ~~Cluster Bombs~~ Freedom!

When people tune into the Conan O'Brien show, home of the masturbating bear, they expect some good ol'-fashioned comedy. When they tune in to the episode with some comedian and Kobe Bryant, they expect good ol'-fashioned comedy and BASKET-BALL. When they tune in to the Conan O'Brien show with Kobe Bryant, and "some comedian" is screaming about illegal drone strikes, torture, 9/11, and Islamophobia, they get mad. They go to message boards. They go to Facebook. They have been betrayed by the most lovable man on the planet: Conan O'Brien. If you are the Conan O'Brien show, you don't ask that comedian back.

The year was 2011. Jamie's dream was to be on *Conan*. After all, it's the comedy he grew up watching. His dad might not "get it" and Allison's parents might like "that Leno fellow" more, but for the authors, this was the only goal. *Conan*.

The booker of the show saw Jamie perform years ago before he started working for Conan. It was in Scotland before the booker was important, which meant none of the other comedians were for much longer sentences for nonviolent drug offenses; the racial profiling programs put in place to curb the drug trade don't work; and drug addiction should be treated as a sickness, not a crime, if the goal is to ever truly reform drug addicts and give them a second chance at normal, healthy, productive lives.

These are things we like to call *facts*. Some of them are even *news*. But even though the hysteria that once surrounded the drug war has somewhat diminished, the media hasn't quite caught up to reporting some of the most significant findings surrounding prohibition.

The Media Is Here to Educate You.
Just Kidding. Here's a Cheech & Chong Clip

Fairness & Accuracy in Reporting, the media watchdog group we've cited extensively in this book, has done a wonderful job cataloging and exposing the media's terrible coverage of the War on Drugs. It's remarkably difficult to find an aggregation of this type, since most criticism of the media's drug coverage either took place in the 1990s or focuses predominately on the Mexican media's silence in covering the War on Drugs.

In 2011, FAIR notes, the Global Commission on Drug Policy, an international panel that assesses the social consequences of the drug war, declared that the "global war on drugs has failed," but only a single network (CBS) reported the findings, and even *that* report included former Bush Sr. drug czar William Bennett chiming in to "reassure viewers that the drug war was in fact working just fine."[9]

In 2012, the Summit of the Americas, a meeting of regional

heads of state, reached the same conclusions as the GCDP. Those calling for decriminalization included Juan Manuel Santos, the right-wing president of Colombia, America's closest regional ally (and drug war collaborator), and even Otto Pérez Molina of Guatemala, School of the Americas graduate and former hard-line general.

Every major network except one limited their coverage of this summit to a Secret Service prostitution scandal that occurred two days before the press arrived in Colombia. The other network, NBC, reported on photos of a beer-drinking Hillary Clinton that were "setting Twitter on fire."

Approaching the election in 2012, FAIR declared, "Very little critical journalism was to be found . . . unless, of course, the story told was one of Mexican cartels rather than U.S. policy."

Even CBS's Norah O'Donnell noted the media's silence on the War on Drugs when she remarked in October 2012: "What about in this election season? It seems like there has been no discussion about this at all. Has there?"[10]

Nope! Unless you count stupid pot jokes.

Like in October 2010, when ABC reported on Prop 19—a ballot initiative on the California statewide ballot to regulate, control, and tax cannabis—and included a clip from *Fast Times at Ridgemont High*; or when *Good Morning America* played a clip of Cheech & Chong in October 2010, and anchor Robin Roberts remarked, "I can't imagine starting a new week talking about the Rolling Stones and the possible legalization of marijuana. It's like the sixties, man."[11]

More recently, CNN's Erin Burnett joked in October 2012 that "some of you have some truly *high* expectations. Mile *high* ones," while *BusinessWest* ran the headline "Joint Venture" in September

2012, and *USA Today* opted for "Ballots Going to Pot" in October 2012.[12]

GET IT?

In reality, it isn't just internet dwellers and citizens of Portland who think the War on Drugs should be ended. A growing constituency of current and former law enforcement agents also believes the program doesn't work, is incredibly wasteful, and should be ended immediately.

That's right. The people who see firsthand just how dangerous drug use is realized that the greater danger lies in prohibition.

Don't Take Our Word for It:
Listen to These Responsible Adults!

The War on Drugs isn't failing because of mismanagement. It's failing because the war was hopeless at its creation. Jack Cole is the executive director of Law Enforcement Against Prohibition (LEAP) and a twenty-six-year veteran of the New Jersey State Police, where he served fourteen years undercover in the Narcotics Bureau. He explained to Allison in a 2009 interview that when the war began to escalate under Nixon in 1970, "people were less likely to die as a result of the drug culture than from falling down the stairs in their own homes or choking to death on food at their own dinner tables." America was at war with a bogeyman—an expensive bogeyman. Cole continued:

> We nor our bosses had any idea of how to fight a war on drugs. Our bosses did know one thing though; they knew how to keep that federal cash-cow being milked in their personal barnyard. To

accomplish that they had to make the drug war appear to be an absolute necessity. So early on we were encouraged to lie about most of our statistics and lie we did.[13]

When the evidence didn't support their claims, Cole explained the cops would routinely exaggerate the amount of drugs they seized by adding the weight of any cutting agents (i.e., lactose, mannitol, starch, or sucrose) found at the scene to the weight of the illegal drug. So a seizure of one ounce of cocaine plus four pounds of lactose would result in a penalty commensurate with the larger amount.

As a consequence of corrupt incentives like these, lots of young people go to jail for bogus offenses. Furthermore, instead of doing good, honest policing, cops are busy inflating drug figures, harassing communities of color, and destroying young people's lives.

There's one area where officers like Cole have had a fair degree of success: the vast increase in arrests for marijuana possession. According to the FBI, marijuana offenses accounted for 48.3 percent of all drug arrests in 2012, averaging out to an arrest every forty-two seconds.[14] But even this "successful" battle in the War on Drugs had unintended consequences.

For example, cracking down on marijuana dealers resulted in those dealers switching to selling harder drugs that were less detectable and far more profitable. Cole claims dealers switched to pushing heroin, methamphetamine, and cocaine, far deadlier drugs. Another "win" for the War on Drugs!

But this doesn't mean the solution is to refocus the war from marijuana to heroin and meth. No, the War on Drugs was doomed to fail at its inception because drug crime doesn't function like other kinds of crime. Cole explains:

> [W]hen officers arrested a robber or rapist, the number of rapes and robberies declines. . . . But when I arrested a drug dealer the number of drug sales didn't change at all. I was simply creating a job opening for a long line of people more than willing to risk arrest for those obscene profits. It was actually worse than that. I wasn't just creating a job opening; I was creating a safe job opening because if they tried to get the job while the dealer was still on the corner he would probably shoot them. I would suggest to you that whole armies of police cannot stop drug trafficking when the profits are this immense.[15]

As for many advocates for ending the War on Drugs, Legalize and Regulate is Cole's mantra. *But won't that cause everyone to use drugs?* you might ask him. Cole has a pretty simple response to that question. "Drugs were not illegal in this country until 1914 and we seemed to get through the first 200 years without that occurring."

Ding!

Just Let Grandma Get High

Aside from the people who enjoy getting high for the sake of getting high, and the people dealing drugs in order to make a living and support their families, there is a third group—sick patients—who need access to illegal drugs in order to ease their pain.

It's difficult to know how many people use medicinal marijuana because the records are sketchy. For example, California does not require residents to register as patients, and of the twenty states (plus the District of Columbia) that allow the medicinal use of cannabis, it is one of only three without such a requirement. California NORML estimates that 1.1 million people are licensed for medical marijuana in that state alone.

But we know there are grandmas like seventy-year-old Betty (not her real name), who told New Jersey's PIX 11 that she has resorted to treating her rare form of liver cancer by buying street pot. She tried going for a marijuana prescription from New Jersey's pot dispensary, but the demand has outgrown supply in the state, and she was unable to legally buy and smoke marijuana.

"Without it, I'd be dead," Betty told PIX. "I couldn't eat, I was throwing up constantly. I lost forty-five pounds." But now able to smoke pot, she has an appetite again and is "healthy enough to have the tumor on her liver removed," the news outlet reports.[16]

Patients like Betty are now forced to stand on the front lines protesting for medicinal marijuana, instead of resting as they should, because the feds are busting into their dispensaries like they're looking for the Taliban.

On the other hand, alcohol—which has its own "dispensaries" called bars, liquor stores, grocery stores, gas stations, et cetera—doesn't help sick people (unless you need to induce vomiting, or your ex-girlfriend who you swore you would never talk to again has the cure to your disease and only alcohol will give you the false courage to call her).

Most things can be done in moderation: drinking, getting high, medicating, eating dessert, you name it. Some people can do the moderation thing, some people can't. The authors can go out and have water all night while watching our friends drink, and wake up at six a.m. to work out. But if you put vegan cake in front of us . . . it's over.

The point is: everyone has their own vices, it is not the government's job to say some vices are okay and some will land individuals a lifetime in jail, especially considering how, oftentimes, the legal vices are more dangerous, more addictive, and easier to buy in bulk.

Of course, there do exist those who can't control their vices and these people are addicts who need help—but prison doesn't help addicts. It sucks them in and spits them back into a society where they are now considered even lesser citizens than when they first entered jail. Now, they may have lost the right to vote, access to public housing, and certain public assistance programs, all because they're sick, and in the United States, sick people are easier to lock up than to help.

Addicts won't get help by making license plates. They need counseling, detox clinics, access to clean needles, and rehab, just as cancer patients need reliable access to medicine that has proven effective and affordable. These demographics represent huge swaths of the drug-using population that could be aided by legalization and free up untold man-hours and budget dollars from law enforcement—not to mention beds in our already overcrowded prisons.

Imagine a world in which the United States would no longer have to arrest 1.9 million people every year for nonviolent drug offenses. And the savings wouldn't stop there. Since 1971, the United States has spent well over $1 trillion on an unwinnable war during a time when our infrastructure is crumbling, and public workers are having their pensions slashed. When the ruling elite claim there just "isn't enough to go around," the War on Drugs is consistently the first program offered up by citizens as an example of wasteful government spending that needs to be cut.

Many current and former law enforcement agents, such as the members of Law Enforcement Against Prohibition, believe the US government should import or produce the drugs and control them for quality, potency, and standardized measurement. Just as individuals died during alcohol prohibition by attempting to concoct "bathtub gin," so individuals now die by experimenting with the potency of drugs. If drugs were monitored by the FDA much as prescription pills are now monitored, overdoses would vastly decline. Then, once the drugs are made legal, the government can tax their sales. That would be one way out of this economic depression.

But can you picture Bill O'Reilly selling that line in prime time? He might have more luck with this:

Drug legalization isn't just a domestic security issue, it also has international implications. Terrorists "make a killing" off prohibition because of the basic principles of economics.

Check this out: In 1997, ten kilograms of reactor-grade plutonium (enough to make an atomic bomb) was valued at $56,000. The "average terrorist" makes his living selling illegal drugs. Heroin, which at the beginning of the War on Drugs in 1970 was valued at $400,000 per kilogram, is still worth $70,000 per kilogram today, despite the immense drop in price caused by the glut of supply created by thirty-seven years of a failed war on drugs. That means the "average terrorist" would have to sell about eight kilograms of pure heroin for every ten kilograms of pure weapons-grade plutonium he wishes to buy. That is not a major problem for the terrorist, as long as we continue the policy of drug prohibition.[17]

But if drug prohibition ended tomorrow, and the government

worked to regulate the drugs, terrorists couldn't sell heroin at the inflated market price. Basically, those "You're funding terrorism" antidrug commercials have inverted reality.

In actuality, it's the US government and its policy of drug prohibition that is aiding the terrorists.

Puff on that.

CHAPTER 8

USA! USA! USA! We're Here to Help . . . with ~~Drones~~ ~~Cluster Bombs~~ Freedom!

When people tune into the Conan O'Brien show, home of the masturbating bear, they expect some good ol'-fashioned comedy. When they tune in to the episode with some comedian and Kobe Bryant, they expect good ol'-fashioned comedy and BASKET-BALL. When they tune in to the Conan O'Brien show with Kobe Bryant, and "some comedian" is screaming about illegal drone strikes, torture, 9/11, and Islamophobia, they get mad. They go to message boards. They go to Facebook. They have been betrayed by the most lovable man on the planet: Conan O'Brien. If you are the Conan O'Brien show, you don't ask that comedian back.

The year was 2011. Jamie's dream was to be on *Conan*. After all, it's the comedy he grew up watching. His dad might not "get it" and Allison's parents might like "that Leno fellow" more, but for the authors, this was the only goal. *Conan*.

The booker of the show saw Jamie perform years ago before he started working for Conan. It was in Scotland before the booker was important, which meant none of the other comedians were hanging off of his balls. Jamie needed a friend, the booker liked his show, and so they bonded.

Years later, this booker got the *Conan* gig and was determined to be the first national television show to book Jamie. This was the one year in Jamie's life where he had "heat," as awful Hollywood people say. He was talking to Letterman and Conan. Letterman may have seemed bigger, but Conan was going to let him do one of his trademark rants, plus Letterman was going to make him wear a suit. Sorry, Dad.

Usually when you audition for a late night show, you submit a seven-minute tape of the exact set you plan to do. The shows receive thousands of auditions, so this is really the only way they can compare talent in a fair and efficient way. *Here is the exact five to seven minutes I'm going to do. Here is the exact time. Those are the exact laughs. Curse words have been taken out. Please, God, book me so I don't have to host at Charlie's Bucket O'Laughs anymore.*

Jamie did not have a TV-ready five minutes. Most of his jokes had the word "cock" in them, and the ones that didn't were about religion or the sponsors of most major TV shows. But also, cock. The booker took such a liking to Jamie and was so kind (crazy?) that he sat through two hours of Jamie's set and found the only five minutes that could work, but more importantly, that still represented Jamie and his politics. He and the authors wanted to make sure you didn't see Jamie out at a club talking about the military-industrial complex, then for his TV debut, talking about his "bitch wife and her dumb period."

They settled on Jamie's rant about torture and drones. Which means: *the most appropriate material Jamie had* was about *torture and drones.*

The authors were flown out to Burbank, California, and the

day of the show we walked to the studio lot and took pictures next to anything that had a *Conan* sign. It was magical. Jamie had a dressing room that was several steps up from the utility closets he's usually shoved into preshow, and the door even had his name on it! Andy Richter was hanging out backstage and interns were trying to catch a glimpse of Kobe.

Jamie didn't care that people were in awe of a superstar basketball player and probably didn't know his name until they read it on the dressing room door. He had Allison and one piece of paper in his pocket: a note given to him by Bill Hicks's mom. Hicks is Jamie's hero, and the only comedian ever to be cut before airing from a late night show for his politics. Jamie had met Mrs. Hicks briefly at the Montreal comedy festival, and she'd given him a small laminated card, a copy of ones handed out at Hicks's funeral with details of his passing on one side, and on the other side a quote: "I left in love and laughter and in truth, and wherever love, laughter, and truth abide, I am there in spirit."

Jamie's pretaping plan was very dramatic and quite cheesy: the authors would walk backstage as the cameras rolled, and then when Conan was introducing Jamie, and shouting out *Citizen Radio*—the show Allison and Jamie had started when they were homeless—Jamie would kiss Allison, who would then move to the side of the stage. Right before he walked onstage, Jamie would read the Bill Hicks card to himself, then walk out and perform his set, which he figured would piss off a few people, just like his hero would have wanted.

Problem was, when you watch *Conan* it looks like the curtains are on a pulley system—as though some crazy TV machine pulls the curtains back to reveal the waving performer to the crowd. But it's not a pulley system. A pulley system would be a fine place to kiss in front of, a fine place to celebrate the end of a decade of struggling—to see a dream come true.

But it is not a pulley system. In fact, it is the two biggest men you've ever seen in your life: two bald giants with terrifying goatees dressed entirely in black. They stand, arms crossed, utterly humorless, holding each side of the curtain. They are the pulley system. And they are not amused by nervous comics looking to have a life moment.

The authors looked at each other. There was no kiss. The spirit of Bill Hicks stayed in Jamie's pocket. Allison timidly waved before being ushered away by the crew.

Jamie took a deep breath. The two sentinels opened the curtain and Jamie walked out to make his television debut. As soon as the crowd cheered, he relaxed.

Surprisingly, his performance went really well. He heard Conan laugh at the joke about torture, and the crowd stayed with him as the rant built to a raging antiwar climax, including a criticism of President Obama's use of drones. This was it. The people were on his side. Fuck this war. Fuck pandering for TV cameras. He had done it.

And the larger media response was great, too. MSNBC's Chris Hayes tweeted that he was shocked something like that got on TV. Journalist Glenn Greenwald also tweeted about it. Jamie was ecstatic. Until he remembered that the world was bigger than his lefty Twitter friends.

Jamie walked backstage, out of breath and with the biggest smile on his face, only to see his big-time agent and manager, both of whom said a version of, "Oh. I didn't know it would, um . . . be so . . . political."

Oh really? Think I should've gone with the period jokes? The agent and manager were promptly fired. Allison and Jamie went back to their hotel. Nothing could ruin this night.

Alas, Conan's Facebook page and website did not get the whole "dream come true" memo. Angry commenters swarmed all over the forums saying things like "I fear Conan will lose anyone to the right of Sean Penn if he keeps playing to the L.A. crowd," and "It was like he was possessed by Keith Olbermann." Jamie didn't understand. He's a comic, not Katniss Everdeen taking down the Capitol.

Coincidentally, Jamie hasn't done stand-up on TV since then. This is what happens when you talk about war. This is what happens even when you talk about an *unpopular* war! It's one thing to make fun of George W. Bush, because that guy is an equal-opportunity idiot. But the concepts of war, and of someone "on our team," a.k.a. Obama, bombing innocent civilians, and of Islamophobia post-9/11 are still too much for some people to handle without getting a poor vegan comedian blackballed for life from his dream job.

Thanks for nothing, America.

But apart from how this incident personally affected Jamie, it's just sad that one of the most important issues of our time can't be talked about by artists if those artists expect to continue getting paid to make their art. The Dixie Chicks were almost sent to Guantánamo after their antiwar comments; Lenny Kravitz was widely criticized for his opposition to the Iraq war (the *New York Post* referred to an exiled Iraqi pop singer who was featured on Kravitz's antiwar song as the "enemy's pal");[1] and Eddie Vedder was the focal point of media criticism for several days following an April 1 concert in which he jumped on a mask of then-president George W. Bush.[2]

That's how little the media tolerates dissent. You can't even jump up and down on a mask of the president without being labeled an enemy combatant.

They Don't Hate Us Because of Our Silky, Shiny Hair

The "it's okay when *our* team does it" attitude is reflected all over America's broader foreign policy. We US citizens are extremely offended if chemical weapons are used in Syria, but we turn a blind eye when our allies use chemical weapons against their enemies (for example, Israel's use of white phosphorus against Palestinians; or Donald Rumsfeld & Co. looking the other way when Saddam Hussein was gassing the Kurds back when the Monster of the Century was still America's friend; or the US funding Egypt's military even while they're beating and murdering activists).

Liberals were outraged when former president Bush ordered the US military to invade and occupy two Muslim countries, but many of them looked the other way when President Obama escalated the war in Afghanistan and killed thousands of individuals, including innocent civilians, with flying death robots.

And the media helps facilitate this kind of reckless hypocrisy by picking and choosing which foreign policy stories are worthy of coverage, and parroting the US government's claim that anyone opposing the United States or its corporate interests must be a terrorist. For example, former NSA boss Michael Hayden compared privacy advocates to terrorists during a August 2013 speech on cybersecurity in Washington.

"They may want to come after the US government, but frankly, you know, the dot-mil stuff is about the hardest target in the

United States," Hayden said, using a shorthand for US military networks. "So if they can't create great harm to dot-mil, who are they going after? Who for them are the World Trade Centers? The World Trade Centers, as they were for al-Qaeda."[3]

But at least Hayden put his name to the smear, unlike several anonymous US officials who offered quotes in a June 2013 *Washington Post* piece about how Edward Snowden's leaks could help the terrorists:

> A second senior intelligence official said there were concerns that disclosure of US surveillance methods would make it easier for terrorist groups to avoid detection. "The more material that gets made public, the more capability we lose," the official said.
>
> Already, several terrorist groups in various regions of the world have begun to change their method of communication based on disclosures of surveillance programs in the media, the official said. He would not elaborate on the communication modes.
>
> "It's frustrating," he said. "Because if they find some other method to communicate, we go dark. And we miss dots. That's not something we're particularly excited about."[4]

So there you have it. Edward Snowden is a terrorist because he made the US government look stupid, and we know that is a fact because the *Washington Post* allows government officials to spout anonymously sourced propaganda in its pages.

To many Americans, it may seem like the world has gone crazy, that for no apparent reason, a majority of the planet seems to irrationally detest the United States just because we have freedom and hope and silky, shiny, well-conditioned hair, and super-awesome teeth. Just because we have *American Idol*, Jeremy Piven, and a terrible remake of *Lone Ranger* . . . and . . . oh my God. Now we hate us too.

Of course, the anger directed at the United States from most of the world extends a bit deeper than hair level (and Jeremy Piven), but we agree that its depth would be difficult for many Americans to determine by casually watching the news. As a regular watcher of prime time American news coverage, you could be forgiven for thinking that every few months, some bearded brown dude gets cheesed off about something, straps dynamite to his chest, and charges into a crowded foreign or domestic marketplace, with the sole aim of "taking down America!" Then the president gets behind a podium, claims "they" hate us for our freedoms, and everyone goes back to eating their TV dinners. DAMN you, bearded people! WHY DO YOU HATE OUR SILKY SMOOTH HAIR?!

And yet, every year, and grossly unreported in the national press, the United States gives billions of dollars in military aid to entirely separate countries for the purpose of violently putting down a resistance in the Arab world that stems largely from Israel seizing Palestinians' land and destroying their homes and killing many of them (many women and children) in the process.

There are a couple reasons the United States gives oodles of cash to Israel. First, they happen to be a geopolitically advantageous ally. Since America is now occupying multiple Middle Eastern countries, it makes sense to have a sturdy ally in that region for stuff like maintaining access to oil reserves and keeping an eye on the Iranians. It's like a tiny war-hungry America, right in the center of all those pesky brown people! Like a little brother who grew up idolizing his bully older sibling and now has spiraled out of control, resulting in our collective imminent doom.

Also, there is a batshit crazy constituency in this country that believes Jesus is going to come back, riding a flying white unicorn and carrying a flaming sword or some shit, and he aims to land in Israel, so all good Christians better have Israel's back in the meantime and look busy, or God is going to be hella mad. If you find yourself agreeing with these right-wing Christian fanatics about all of those evil Palestinians, remember that these are the same bunch who believe gay people cause hurricanes.

So the crazy Jewish people team up with the crazy Christian people, unaware of (or conveniently ignoring) the fact that their Jesus-loving allies believe that after their joint work is done, the Jews are going to burn in hell for eternity, since they didn't believe the Jesus is going to come back to earth on a flying unicorn thing. Weird partnership.

Seriously, this is how foreign policy gets crafted. These crazy religious people form partnerships with lobbying groups like the American Israel Public Affairs Committee (AIPAC), who then ask the US government for more money in aid.

In order to understand what's got the world so pissed off at America, let's imagine the following scenario:

You and a group of your friends are kicking it one Friday night at your friend Amirah's house. Everyone is having a great time. There's music and Chex Mix. CHEX MIX!!

You are America. You've got a lot going for you. You're loaded, got a sweet-ass pad, TONS of Chex Mix, and life is pretty great. You've invited your friends: Canada, Mexico, the UK (nice, but won't stop saying "cheers"), Australia, who brought shrimp because GET IT??

Anyway, that's when your cell phone starts buzzing and you see it's your BEST FRIEND IN THE WORLD, Esther, calling.

"YOU GUYS! IT'S ESTHER!" you declare, "IMMA INVITE HER OVER!"

To which, the entire room—everyone—cries, "Noooo! NOT ESTHER!"

See, Esther has some socializing issues.

Whenever she joins a party, Esther immediately acts like she owns the place. She rudely hogs the Chex Mix, and one time, she even tried to annex Amirah's entire home. Weird, right?

Weird, and unpleasant. Also, sometimes Esther asks you for money. Like, a lot of money. Like, billions of dollars a year. I know! Crazy. And you're all, "Um, Esther? I don't think I should give you money when you're stealing everyone's Chex Mix," and she's all, "I thought we were friends!" and then she starts crying, and you end up giving her all your Chex Mix, plus your savings.

Ugh, but that's what friends are for, right?

"Please! NOT ESTHER!" the room cries again, but alas, it's too late. You've already texted your BFF 4 Life and told her to come on over.

Fifteen minutes later, Esther has kicked down the front door, thrown white phosphorus on your friends, and seized the living room as her colony. Amirah tries to throw a Cheez Ball at Esther at one point, and then Esther starts screaming about how she was only defending herself from retaliatory snack food launches.

You try to sneak out the back door, and you're pretty sure everyone is super pissed at you . . . and maybe dead. Everyone is pissed or dead.

Aaaanyway, Esther is Israel, guys.

We realize now we probably should have gotten this disclaimer out of the way before making this analogy. So here goes: WE LIKE JEWS!

One of the authors is a sort-of Jew himself! The other married a sort-of Jew, which means she's got to like them a little bit, or she is part of some elaborate undercover operation to take down the Jews one skinny comedian at a time. Either way, at least one of us LOVES the Jews and his Jewish family.

The authors don't like Nazis, skinheads, using the word "Jew" aggressively at the end of a sentence, saying things like, "does it smell like a Jew was here?," and so on.

The Jews have an incredible liberal history that you would all probably really dig. It is an amazing story about overcoming huge obstacles (like, say, genocide) and inspiring the world with massive feats of bravery. The majority of Jews in America are extremely liberal, and Jewish people played huge supportive roles in the civil rights movement. Long story, short: WE HAVE JEWISH FRIENDS.

Okay. Everyone got that?

This seems like a childish thing to point out, but there is this trend in America implemented by very well-organized, well-connected lobbying groups like AIPAC that goes like this: if you say something like "I wish Israel didn't kill that Palestinian kid today," AIPAC claims what you really mean is "I love Hitler and admire his work."

It is a very sad, bizarre, and real fear among dissidents that, if you happen to criticize Israel, you will be framed as being anti-Semitic. Many media figures, from raging skinhead Alice Walker and PBS's Bill Moyers, to author Norman Finkelstein (whose parents were Holocaust survivors!), have been labeled anti-Semitic or worse for wanting nothing more than for Israel to abide by international law. Finkelstein, whose attackers call him a Holocaust denier and self-loathing Jew (another favorite smear), says the reason he defends Palestinian rights is because of lessons his mother taught him *from her experience in the Holocaust.*

AIPAC and groups like it are using the fear of the Holocaust and anti-Semitism to put American Jews (primarily elderly American Jews) into lifelong fear paralysis, which is way more offensive than dissidents asking Israel not to bomb children. Using the Holocaust as propaganda to then turn around and systematically kill and torture another people is hypocritical, gross, and wrong.

So that's that. We don't hate the Jews. Moving on.

Seriously, We *Do Not Hate Jews,* but We Have Some More Thoughts About This

If you watch the news in the United States, it may seem as though Israel was just hanging out, feeding homeless orphans, when devil-horned Hamas rose up from the sand covered in bombs, kicked down the wall, and started shooting millions of rockets while screaming, "WE HATE HOMELESS ORPHANS!" and killing everyone in sight.

In reality, Hamas is a democratically elected Palestinian political group. Every once in a while, Hamas will launch a rocket into Israel, which, by the way, is totally inexcusable and severely uncool. Why are they launching rockets? Well, some of them are assholes. We aren't fans of Hamas. In fact, we were huge fans of the fact that, not too long ago, Palestine was becoming way more secular. However, when your homes are being bulldozed, your food and water access restricted, your children are being killed, and there is 50 percent unemployment, if a bunch of dudes with guns show up and say they are going to make your lives better, you are probably going to give them a chance. Do we agree with violence? Of course not, but look at what America did when we were attacked on September 11. We bombed everybody. Like, everybody. Compare that to some shitty rockets that barely work.

Any life lost is a tragedy, and it's important to remember that when discussing the Israel-Palestine issue, but it's also essential to keep something called "proportionality" in mind.

This concept eludes otherwise liberal-minded people because Democrats and Republicans have been unified on the "Israel front" for so long. Few politicians have the audacity to challenge the powerful Jewish lobbying group AIPAC out of fear of being labeled anti-Semitic. In reality, there is nothing anti-Jewish about wanting Israel to stop killing Palestinians and get along with its neighbors. If anything, achieving peace with Palestinians ensures the long-term safety of Israel, and it also helps achieve the whole not-killing-children objective.

There are way, way, WAY more Palestinians dying in this conflict than Israelis, probably because Israel has the second-greatest army in the world, which is really just the US Military 2.0, thanks to our billions of dollars in subsidization. Starting to see why the Arabs are mad yet? We would be pretty mad if Esther, er, Israel killed, like, everybody we know.

#Newsfail exacerbates this problem by warping Americans' perspectives about what's happening overseas. For example, the United Nations' High Commissioner for Human Rights released a report in March 2013 tallying the extent of death and destruction from Israel's attacks on the Gaza Strip in November 2012. The fighting killed over 174 Palestinians in Gaza, including 33 children and 13 women. Six Israelis were killed.[5]

These reports are not coming from "Noam Chomsky's Daily Zine," but from the United Nations, well-respected human rights groups inside and outside of Israel, and Israeli press—which incidentally does a better job of covering Israel's crimes than the US media.

Yet, as national media watch group Fairness & Accuracy in Reporting points out, the headlines the media generated on this issue focused on one child in Gaza, eleven-month-old Omar al-Masharawi, and the claim that he was *not* killed by Israelis:

"UN Ties Gaza Baby's Death to Palestinians," the *New York Times* chose as its headline.

"UN: Palestinian Militants Likely Killed Gaza Baby," cried the AP, and referred to a photo of Omar's body being held by his father, BBC cameraman Jihad al-Masharawi, as "an image that became a symbol of what Palestinians said was Israeli aggression."[6]

FAIR clarifies that this is not a "he said, she said" situation, and what Palestinians "said was Israeli aggression" *was actually* Israeli aggression, but who is checking the FAIR website on a regular basis? Typical Americans are left with typical coverage from the establishment media.

Not even a massacre is called a massacre.

Nor is hypocrisy reported as hypocrisy. In September 2013, the *New York Times* published an article about a Human Rights Watch report charging Syria's government with the use of cluster bombs, a "widely prohibited weapon."[7]

Now, cluster bombs are nasty things. They're basically flying land mines, and any regime using them is guilty of violating the Convention on Cluster Munitions, which has been signed by 112 countries.

Buried in the eighth paragraph of the eleven-paragraph *New York Times* article is the fact that eighty-five countries have *not* signed the convention, including the United States, Syria, and Israel.

In fact, FAIR reports that the United States has actually used cluster bombs in places like Serbia, Afghanistan, Iraq, and Yemen.

This is the height of hypocrisy: when our enemies use these weapons, they're terrorists, but when the United States and its allies use them, they're considered reasonable uses of force.

Furthermore, the media often simply parrots whatever information is handed to them by the US military—without independently verifying that, for example, the victims were not merely innocent bystanders. FAIR explored this phenomenon by examining just a couple of headlines about a drone strike that killed "six suspected militants in Yemen."

REUTERS: "DRONE STRIKE KILLS SIX
SUSPECTED MILITARY IN YEMEN."

CNN.COM: "MORE SUSPECTED AL-QAEDA MILITANTS
KILLED AS DRONE STRIKES INTENSIFY IN YEMEN."[8]

But how, you might wonder, can anyone at Reuters who is not on the ground at the strike site actually know who is being killed and whether or not they are "militants," which sounds like an apt term for people who deserve to die under a flying death robot's steely gaze?

Here's how that works: Thanks to a report by the *New York Times*, we know that the White House policy for who is considered a "militant" is "all military-age males in a strike zone."[9] This seems to us like a pretty wide net for selecting HUMAN TARGETS for elimination.

It's like the most lethal game of chicken-and-egg ever played. If you are a military-age male standing in the strike zone, then you are a "militant." And if you are a "militant," you are a worthy target for a drone strike and can find your way on to what has become known as President Obama's "Kill List."

That's bad enough, but then the government turns to the media and says, "That smoking corpse was a terrorist," and very few newspaper editors pause to wonder *Is that strictly true?* before printing it on the front page. Some journalists, like Jeremy Scahill in his book *Dirty Wars*, bother to actually visit these remote places where drone strikes killed "militants," and interview the farmers in the area, which is when we learn the so-called militants were actually civilians, or farmers, or kids.

Oopsie!

The media also tends to adopt the US government's line of thinking that drone strikes can defeat terrorism. In a June 2012 article in the *New York Times*, Declan Walsh and Eric Schmitt write on the apparent drone killing of al-Qaeda "deputy leader" Abu Yahya al-Libi:

> If his death is borne out this time, it would be a milestone in a covert eight-year airstrike campaign that has infuriated Pakistani officials but that has remained one of the United States' most effective tools in combating militancy.[10]

But drones also serve to radicalize the local population, and al-Qaeda uses drone strikes as its biggest recruiting tool, so in actuality, drone strikes don't "combat militancy."

Drone strikes *promote* militancy.

Farea al-Muslimi, a Yemeni writer and activist, spoke movingly before the Senate Judiciary Committee about a drone attack on his village that took place in April 2013.

> In the past, what Wessab's villagers knew of the US was based on my stories about my wonderful experiences here. The friendships and values I experienced and described to the villagers helped them understand the America that I know and that I love. Now, however, when they think of America, they think of the terror they feel from the drones that hover over their heads, ready to fire missiles at any time. What the violent militants had previously failed to achieve, one drone strike accomplished in an instant. There is now an intense anger against America in Wessab.
>
> This is not an isolated incident. The drone strikes are the face of America to many Yemenis. I have spoken to many victims of US drone strikes, like a mother in Jaar who had to identify her innocent eighteen-year-old son's body through a video in a stranger's cell phone, or the father in Shaqra who held his four- and six-year-old children as they died in his arms.[11]

Intense stuff. But as FAIR notes, US broadcast networks and cable channels ignored this story, which isn't surprising given that al-Muslimi's remarks fly in the face of the claim that drone strikes are surgical and sterile instruments that prevent civilians from being hurt, and they work to combat terror.

Here was a real-life Yemenite saying, *Actually, that's not true. Civilians die all the time, and the drone strikes are turning people against the United States.*

And there seems to be no room for that message on the corporate airwaves. It's like, why consult the experts on an issue involving specialized knowledge? I know, whenever I'm building a dam or skyscraper, I bring in my Aunt Helen even though she might not have "engineering experience." Likewise, when discussing Yemeni drone strike victims, I talk to John Boehner.

Don't Get Us Started on Iran

Iran has proved to be the mainstream media's perfect storm of atrocious reporting because it combines hagiographies of Israel with reports from frequently anonymous government officials.

And that's in an ideal situation. Sometimes the media can't even get basic facts right. In an October 2013 issue of *Time* magazine, in an article titled "Iran's Dubious Charms," the magazine ran a graphic featuring a timeline of the "history of hostility" between the United States and Iran, except they missed a few spots.[12]

For example, 1953, when the United States helped orchestrate a coup that ousted Iranian prime minister Mohammed Mossadegh. Or the United States's support for Iraqi dictator Saddam Hussein in the war with Iran, including Iraqi chemical weapons attacks on Iran, or when a United States cruiser shot down Iran Air flight 655 in 1988, killing 290 passengers on board.

Devoting a little column space to those events might help Americans understand why there are tensions between the two countries that lie somewhere between silky hair envy and nuclear bombs.

In an October 2013 *Washington Post* report, David Nakamura and William Booth permitted an Israeli official to anonymously (and ominously) warn Americans that they can't trust Iranians:

"The Persians have been using these tactics for thousands of years, before America came to be."[13]

Anonymity is only supposed to be granted in very rare instances, precisely so government officials can't use the cloak of anonymity to spout propagandist lies about their opponents, ramification-free.

But sometimes the media doesn't even bother with anonymity to unleash baseless, frequently bigoted claims against those perceived as exotic "others."

"Islamists . . . lack the mental equipment to govern," the *New York Times*'s David Brooks wrote in a July 2013 column. "Incompetence is built into the intellectual DNA of radical Islam."[14]

When fear and bigotry are the default setting of many in the news business, it's no wonder the media gets the Iran story so wrong, so consistently.

In 2013, NBC got what they treated as a huge scoop: Iran's new president said his country isn't interested in a nuclear bomb. *Holy. Shit.*

The news exploded as though President Rouhani had made some unprecedented proclamation. But in fact, this has been Iran's default position for decades.

In 1991, Iranian vice president and head of the Atomic Energy Organization of Iran Reza Amrollahi said, "Our objective in promoting nuclear industries is merely its peaceful use."[15]

Iranian president Hashemi Rafsanjani said in March 1997: "We're not after nuclear bombs and we won't go after biological and chemical weapons."[16]

Supreme Leader Ayatollah Sayyid Ali Khamenei said in 2003: "The statement that the Islamic Republic wants to obtain chemical weapons and the atomic bomb is totally false."[17]

There are literally dozens of these examples, right up to 2012, when then-Iranian president Mahmoud Ahmadinejad said the country had no plans to develop a nuclear weapon.

But according to a 2012 CNN/Gallup poll, three quarters of Americans believed at that time that Iran already had a nuclear weapon, and about 80 percent believed that it either had one or would get one in short order.[18]

Why do Americans have such a poor understanding of foreign policy?

A large part of the problem is the media's obsession with portraying Iran as a dangerous, unhinged foe. In a 2013 poll conducted by the *New York Times* and CBS, people were asked a very odd question: would they support military action against Iran "in order to prevent them from producing a nuclear weapon?"[19]

The question itself is misleading; it assumes that an attack would prevent Iran from acquiring nukes—end of story. But there's no way an air assault would destroy Iran's *knowledge* of nuclear technology and therefore its ability to, say, retaliate against an unprovoked attack *with* a nuclear bomb.

Despite such clear logic found in the pages of our humble book, the media is accustomed to the narrative that bombing leads to peace, simply because the US military and government officials claim it's so.

And US citizens (and the people in other countries on the receiving end of the US military and our weapons) suffer the consequences. When the media parrots propaganda unquestioningly, fails to acknowledge the results of blowback, and refuses to report on the horrific acts of our allies, it does a disservice to the American people, but it also makes the world a much more dangerous place.

Full Circle: Eleven Years After the Iraq Invasion, the United States Is Still Bombing the Rest of the World, but At Least *Citizen Radio* Exists Now!

Okay. We're aware that's cold comfort (particularly if you're an Iraqi, or Afghan, or Pakistani, or Iranian, or Syrian, or . . . *trails off in tears*).

But the rise of independent media is no small feat, and it will play a significant role in the changing world. Alternative media is essential if we're ever going to challenge and modify the existing narrative that hyper-capitalism is the only valid economic model, unending war is just a fact of life, and governments and corporations will continue to exploit poor people and pollute the environment all over the world.

It's been eleven years since the US-led invasion of Iraq, and our country is still at war, still occupying vast swaths of the planet, with no signs of rolling back its military aggression even though Americans have, time and time again, expressed their war fatigue, and interest in addressing domestic issues like job creation and living wages.

And the media has largely been complicit in reinforcing that messaging, primarily by limiting the scope of debate on its networks, and between its columns. Shocker: John McCain has not yet called for "the people's uprising" during one of his eight million *Meet the Press* appearances.

Americans can't make informed decisions if all they're offered is #newsfail, which is why it's going to take alternative media to challenge their narrative and reshape the national dialogue. Just like many Americans' bodies have become unhealthy sustaining themselves on high-caloric processed foods, so their minds have become stagnant, crammed with propagandist government memos via the major networks.

Citizen Radio is one small step in the alternative media revolution, but change is coming. The days of the media empire are numbered, as long as places like the internet are kept open, fair, and uncensored, and all communities expand net access so every global citizen has an opportunity to make their voice heard.

Once Americans are educated, then they have the tools to do what we always say at the end of every *Citizen Radio* episode:

"Turn off your radio and fuck shit up."

EPILOGUE

Save the Tote Bags!: Why Independent Media
Is Essential to Saving Democracy and the World

Citizen Radio and its hosts have come a long way from living out of our car and interviewing Ralph Nader in a bathtub. True, the bar was pretty low, but it's like the old adage says: "If you fail for the first ten years, and set the bar at the pits of hell, then there is nowhere to go but up!"

The authors started *Citizen Radio* not caring about making money or even furthering our careers. We had stories that we wanted to tell. Stories centered around the poverty divide, institutional racism, and the pandemic of rape culture. What we didn't count on was that the stories we cared about so deeply really couldn't be found anywhere else. Nobody was calling Noam Chomsky for interviews on CNN. Because of our commitment to unbiased, truthful reporting and giving airtime to the voices that can't otherwise get heard, *Citizen Radio* has attracted an army of so-called Maniacs from around the world, including Noam himself.

Week by week, month by month, year by year, *Citizen Radio*

has expanded its reach. From our humble beginnings, we now have been downloaded millions of times from tens of thousands of unique listeners in the United States, Canada, the United Kingdom, Australia, Germany, Japan, France, China, South Korea, and dozens of other countries on almost every continent. Many of our listeners have gone on to do amazing things like starting protest groups of their own, including Occupy chapters, and advocating for progressivism in their daily lives whether they work at a co-op, in the military, or in the case of one Maniac, in the Pentagon. Even though we were broadcasting from our shitty apartment, our equipment resting on an IKEA children's table and cats sitting on our laps, people listened. To us, the show seemed almost fake. Like we were recording it for ourselves.

Which may have been the secret to our success.

Citizen Radio is a 100 percent listener-supported show. We have no corporate sponsors. That means we're free to criticize big business as it pollutes the earth, consumes resources, and abuses workers. Unlike other networks that take millions of dollars from Wall Street institutions, we're able to speak truth to power, as opposed to dancing around issues in order to secure another ad revenue check.

In 2011, we decided to take the grand experiment a little further: to see what would happen if *Citizen Radio* brought the same combination of news, weird cat stories, and weird guests to a live audience.

Would people get off their couches to attend?

As it turned out, yes, yes they would.

Citizen Radio Live! recorded for the first time on March 2011 in Manhattan's Chelsea neighborhood at the Upright Citizens Brigade Theatre—the only theater *Citizen Radio* feels comfortable in, probably because there's duct tape on the seats, and one time we saw a roach that we thought was a rat almost attack Mike Birbiglia. It also has a rich comedy history. During the 2008 writers' strike, the casts of *30 Rock*, *Saturday Night Live*, and *The Colbert Report* performed live shows at the UCB to raise money for the strikers. They could have sold out Carnegie Hall if they wanted to, but they came to the UCB because of its heart and soul.

Every *CR Live* show included an insane lineup of big-name guests because the authors assumed no one in their right mind would pay actual dollars to see us (primarily because we are self-loathing artists). But we assumed if we loaded a show with famous people, New Yorkers would pay to see *those* guys and be stuck listening to *Citizen Radio* in the process. Suckers.

Over the course of a handful of shows, *CR* had guests like Sarah Silverman, Matt Taibbi, Jeremy Scahill, Moby, Billy Connolly, Janeane Garofalo, Melissa Harris-Perry, Amy Goodman, and musical performances by Regina Spektor and Reggie Watts. It was really cool to see an alternative comedy audience blend with serious political folks, and to witness everyone cry along to stories about Afghanistan, and see progressive intellectuals laugh at dick jokes.

The first show featured Scahill, Taibbi, and Garofalo. Amy Goodman—host of *Democracy Now!*, which careful readers will remember as the whole reason the authors got into independent media in the first place—and the staff of Bill Moyers's television show were in the crowd, and in case we weren't nervous enough, so was Jamie's dad. Fun fact: Jamie didn't actually know Amy Goodman was there until midway into a rant when he yelled the word "cocksucker" and accidently made direct eye contact with her, Amy Goodman, the most important news voice of our time.

Luckily, Amy laughed!

And Jamie's dad did not rush the stage to lecture him about his potty mouth.

That was the first moment the authors knew the live show could be something special. Not only was it oversold, with people having to sit on the floor and stand in the back, but Scahill and Taibbi had never met before that night! With all the news shows in the world, our little podcast was the first to bring these two journalistic giants together. Not only that, but they were kind of nervous. Both of them asked us if it was a requirement to be funny, and if they should prepare material. To us, they were gods, single-handedly taking down Wall Street and mercenary groups before breakfast. But for them, in the land of comedy, they were worried about looking like fuckups. Celebs: they're just like us!

The show was great and the guests were smart and funny, and apparently the authors were charming enough that Jamie's dad didn't "accidently" say something passive-aggressive after the show. Only that he was proud.

Since then, *Citizen Radio* has received thousands of emails from young activists who found inspiration from our little start-up podcast, and have gone out into the world to change it for the better, whether that means coming out to their parents, starting a school petition or their own alternative media outlet, or running for office.

So here's what we've learned on our quest to bring democracy into your headphones on a daily basis: The people whose voices matter the most are also the least likely to get heard. When you turn on the news, it's the same old rich white people that have systematically ruined this country regurgitating the same tired, stale ideas. And they keep getting invited back! Paid cable news pundits have started wars and sunk the economy. *Meet the Press* would rather pull up a chair for the ghost of Ronald Reagan than bring on a poor person as a guest—let alone a cat!

The Internet Is Ours—Keep It Neutral

A big part of keeping diverse voices (and cats!) in independent media and on the internet is keeping the web a democratic zone, equally accessible to all its users—a.k.a. net neutrality.

Net neutrality, or NN, is the idea that internet service providers and governments should treat all data on the internet equally, and shouldn't discriminate or charge differently depending on the user, content, or website. In other words, CNN's website shouldn't download at a faster rate just because they're CNN, their content is "approved," and they can afford to pay more for faster download rates from their internet service provider, while a little website like *Citizen Radio* lags in speed because we're pinko commie lefties that pay our cable bill in quarters we dug out of the duct-taped seats at UCB.

For years, NN advocates have been fighting to require the government to protect the internet's democratic space by law, particularly because some US leaders have shown strong interest in monitoring and censoring the internet, as is commonplace in countries like China, Saudi Arabia, and North Korea. Do you want to live in China, Saudi Arabia, or North Korea? No? Then listen up.

Anti-NN lawmakers are fond of using words like "cyberattacks" in support of their desire to monitor and control your use of the internet. You don't want terrorists emerging from some wormhole in your laptop and taking over your bedroom like Airbnb, right? Of course you don't! Look, while Chinese hackers and groups like

Anonymous certainly exist, let's just say that any government official using them as an excuse to crack down on internet freedom is making a specious argument at best—and at worst, a very dangerous one.

The mainstream media in this country already functions on many levels as a willfully ignorant propaganda machine—trust us, you don't want to hand over the internet to the government or we'll all be reading from the one government-approved website that tells us every day that everything is going super awesome, nothing to see here, move along, as a giant Uncle Sam GIF smiles and waves.

But hey, despite decades of imperialism gone wild, hypercapitalism, widespread poverty, and vanishing civil liberties, there is some good news.

Independent media and with it, direct action, are on the rise—which is a good thing because the only ways for the little people to fight back are through collective organizing and circumventing an establishment media collared and leashed by its corporate overlords.

One of the catalysts for the surge in independent broadcasting outlets like *Citizen Radio* was the revelation of the Bush administration's heinous and self-serving lies to the American people about those pesky "Weapons of Mass Destruction," and the media acting as an accomplice to those lies. Blogs like *Daily Kos*, *Firedoglake*, and *RedState* surged in popularity because consumers realized they weren't getting the full truth from their government and mainstream media.

Bloggers at these sites made names for themselves by digging deeper into mainstream media stories. For example, in 2009 Marcy Wheeler from the blog *emptywheel* reported that Khalid Sheikh Mohammed was waterboarded 183 times in one month, a figure well above the frequency (and with a greater volume of water) than the CIA rules permit.[1] And it was a former blogger, Glenn Greenwald, who blew the door off the NSA spying scandal in 2013 when he met a young whistle-blower named Edward Snowden.

And following the election of President Obama, alternative media became even more essential when it became clear that the media's idea of "balance" is networks like MSNBC ("home of progressives") largely toeing the administration's line and refusing to criticize the president on issues like NSA spying, failing to close Guantánamo, and escalating drone strikes and the occupation of Afghanistan.

As discussed, one of the most popular vehicles for alternative media is the internet, which is why it's essential that we fight to keep the web open and available to all independent media outlets.

You might be thinking, *Oh Allison, oh Jamie, aren't you guys being just a* touch *reactionary here? I mean, really, I know the government is coming after my guns but do you think they actually want to take away my AOL Instant Messenger and hike up my cable rates, too? That seems so silly!*

Okay, first of all, the government is NOT COMING FOR YOUR GUNS. Jesus, didn't you read chapter 6?

But you might be surprised to learn that as recently as the fall of 2013, amid the heated debate over the Affordable Care Act, House Republicans put together a proposal of demands, one of which included, bizarrely, a block on net neutrality.[2] Yep, they did that.

Massive internet service providers (ISPs) are also against NN. For example, Verizon filed a lawsuit against the FCC challenging NN rules back in 2011 that, in September 2013, finally made it into the US Court of Appeals in DC.

Verizon calls the FCC's 2011 internet rules that require internet providers to treat all web traffic equally "excessive," and an "arbitrary and capricious intrusion which violates the company's right to free speech." Because, remember, according to *Citizens United*, corporations are people entitled to protection of "speech," which also apparently means "business decisions." Verizon sees a great opportunity in burning NN rules because there's a huge potential boon for them in tiered access. Big companies capable of paying through the nose for faster internet speed will pay that money to Verizon.

In 2014, Verizon won a victory from a federal appeals court that will allow the carrier to charge extra fees for speedier delivery of online content. Edward Wyatt of the *New York Times* noted it is now conceivable ISPs will be able to "offer Internet content providers—ESPN or Facebook, for example—faster service to deliver their content to consumers, at a price."[3]

The debate behind Verizon's lawsuit is: should the government be responsible for keeping the internet a level playing field?

The answer is yes, because the internet isn't just a leisure tool. It's where Americans get vital information. According to a 2012 Pew poll, more Americans get their news online than from radios or newspapers.[4] So at its heart, NN isn't an antibusiness concept—NN is anticensorship.

The internet has to remain an open, democratic space so Americans can make news consumption decisions not based on their cable provider's economic prowess, but based on their independent will.

And for consumers who saw the value of alternative media in exposing the Bush administration's lies, or highlighting President Obama's expanding wars in Afghanistan and flying death robots, NN should be a principal concern.

Another monumental moment in the battle for NN unfolded

in February 2014 when Netflix caved to payment demands made by Comcast, the country's largest cable and broadband provider. Essentially, Netflix paid to gain faster and more reliable access to Comcast's subscribers. Sadly, the Comcast-Netflix precedent didn't end there.

Proponents of a democratic internet were dealt yet another blow in April 2014 when the Federal Communications Commission proposed new rules that will allow ISPs to sell faster pipes into people's homes to companies willing to pay through the nose for it. Put simply: if implemented, these rules will create an internet that will no longer be an equal playing field because those companies with the most money can simply buy the fastest internet speeds.

"The FCC is inviting ISPs to pick winners and losers online," Michael Weinberg, vice president at Public Knowledge, a Washington-based consumer-advocacy group, said in a statement. "This is not Net Neutrality. This standard allows ISPs to impose a new price of entry for innovation on the Internet."[5]

"This is not Net Neutrality," Craig Aaron, president and CEO of Free Press, a group that champions internet openness, concurred in a statement. "It's an insult to those who care about preserving the open Internet to pretend otherwise. The FCC had an opportunity to reverse its failures and pursue real Net Neutrality by reclassifying broadband under the law. Instead, in a moment of political cowardice and extreme shortsightedness, it has chosen this convoluted path that won't protect Internet users."

As of this writing, Free Press is asking FCC chairman Tom Wheeler to throw out the proposed rules.

The internet is ours. From its genesis, the internet was a government project funded by US taxpayer dollars. It does not belong to private corporations, yet companies like Verizon want to make it their own and profit from it. Think about it this way: you don't pay Tom Brokaw's salary. But the advertisers on NBC *Nightly News* sure do. And among those advertisers are . . . you guessed it: Verizon.

In Conclusion

In the years to come, we hope to expand *Citizen Radio* and reach more little progressives bursting with energy in their conservative communities. The goal of the show is to create a family for the disenfranchised, so they can organize and fight back, and that entails finding the marginalized and inviting them into the fold.

Like *Democracy Now*, the *Majority Report*, and Bill Moyers, *Citizen Radio* wants to challenge the "very serious people" who keep leading the country into disaster after disaster, and that requires the creation of an alternate narrative to government and corporate media propaganda.

#Newsfail isn't inevitable. You, a media consumer, have the ability to turn off CNN and seek out independent media on the internet. Don't worry about abandoning the mainstream media.

They (and Wolf Blitzer's beard) will be just fine.

NOTES

Introduction: #NEWSFAIL: None of the News That's Fit to Print

1. Tom Shales, "A Media Role in Selling the War? No Question," *Washington Post*, April 25, 2007: http://www.washingtonpost.com/wp-dyn/content/article /2007/04/24/AR2007042402444.html.

2. nbcnews.com/id/4260074/ns/msnbc-the_ed_show#.UxD7nnddVhw.

Chapter 1: Jon Stewart Shrugged: How a Comedy Program Became the Most Trusted Name in "News"

1. Fairness & Accuracy in Reporting, "CNN vs. SiCKO," July 11, 2007: http://fair.org/take-action/action-alerts/cnn-vs-sicko/.

2. FAIR, "CNN vs. SiCKO."

3. Bill Moyers, "Buying the War," *Bill Moyers Journal*, April 25, 2007: http:// www.pbs.org/moyers/journal/btw/transcript1.html.

4. Jon Stewart on *Fox News Sunday*, June 2011.

5. Liz Halloran, "Glenn Beck Comes to D.C., Controversy Follows," NPR, August 27, 2010: http://www.npr.org/templates/story/story.php?storyId =129449408.

6. "Rally to Restore Sanity" Facebook page, October 30, 2010: https://www .facebook.com/events/118856078167623.

7. "The Maddow/Stewart interview, uncut," *The Rachel Maddow Show*, November 12, 2010: http://www.msnbc.com/rachel-maddow-show/the-maddow stewart-interview-uncut.

8. Matt Cherette, "*The Daily Show* on Occupy Wall Street: Shoot the

Messenger," *Gawker*, October 19, 2011: http://gawker.com/5851164/the
-daily-show-on-occupy-wall-street-shoot-the-messenger.

9. Neal Broverman, "Jon Stewart: Glitter Bombers Act Like Petulant Children," *Advocate*, February 17, 2012: http://www.advocate.com/comedy
/2012/02/17/john-stewart-glitter-bombers-act-petulant-children.

Chapter 2: Get Your Flaming Arrows Ready: Class War and the Media That Mocks Protesters Fighting It

1. Henry Blodget, "Erin Burnett Is Vapid—The Wall Street Protests Matter," *Business Insider*, October 5, 2011: http://www.businessinsider.com/erin
-burnett-is-vapid-the-wall-street-protests-matter-2011-10.

2. Andrew Ross Sorkin, "On Wall Street, a Protest Matures," *New York Times*, October 3, 2011: http://dealbook.nytimes.com/2011/10/03/on-wall-street
-a-protest-matures.

3. Ginia Bellafante, "Gunning for Wall Street, With Faulty Aim," *New York Times*, September 23, 2011: http://www.nytimes.com/2011/09/25/nyregion
/protesters-are-gunning-for-wall-street-with-faulty-aim.html?_r=3&hp&.

4. Allison Kilkenny, "Correcting the Abysmal 'New York Times' Coverage of Occupy Wall Street," *Nation*, September 26, 2011: http://www.thenation
.com/blog/163626/correcting-abysmal-new-york-times-coverage-occupy
-wall-street.

5. Andrew Ross Sorkin, "Occupy Wall Street: A Frenzy That Fizzled," *New York Times*, September 17, 2012: http://dealbook.nytimes.com/2012/09/17
/occupy-wall-street-a-frenzy-that-fizzled.

6. Sorkin, "On Wall Street, a Protest Matures."

7. Erin Burnett, *OutFront*, CNN, October 3, 2011: http://transcripts.cnn
.com/TRANSCRIPTS/1110/03/ebo.01.html.

Chapter 3: Al Gore Is Fat and We're All Going to Die: Or, You Can't Blame Climate Change on Vegans

1. Ian Burrell, "Has Rupert Murdoch Turned Into a Climate Change Sceptic?" *Independent*, January 11, 2013: http://www.independent.co.uk
/news/media/press/has-rupert-murdoch-turned-into-a-climate-change
-sceptic-8448688.html.

2. Jill Fitzsimmons and Jocelyn Fong, "STUDY: Climate Coverage Plummets on Broadcast Networks," *Media Matters*, April 16, 2012: http://

mediamatters.org/research/2012/04/16/study-climate-coverage-plummets
-on-broadcast-ne/184103.

3. Max Greenberg, "Reuters Climate Change Coverage Declined Significantly After 'Skeptic' Editor Joined," *Media Matters*, July 23, 2013:
http://mediamatters.org/blog/2013/07/23/reuters-climate-change-coverage
-declined-signif/195015.

4. Ben Dimiero, "FOXLEAKS: Fox boss ordered staff to cast doubt on climate
science," *Media Matters*, December 15, 2010: http://mediamatters.org
/blog/2010/12/15/foxleaks-fox-boss-ordered-staff-to-cast-doubt-o/174317.

5. Paul Steinhauser, "CNN Poll: Do Americans agree with Obama on climate change and immigration?" *CNN.com*, January 22, 2013: http://
politicalticker.blogs.cnn.com/2013/01/22/cnn-poll-do-americans-agree
-with-obama-on-climate-change-and-immigration.

6. Andrew Breiner, "New Infographic: The Anti-Science Climate Denier Caucus," *ThinkProgress*, July 11, 2013: http://thinkprogress.org/climate/2013
/07/11/2289051/new-infographic-the-anti-science-climate-denier-caucus.

7. Felicity Carus, "UN urges global move to meat and dairy-free diet," *Guardian*, June 2, 2010: http://www.theguardian.com/environment/2010/jun/02
/un-report-meat-free-diet.

8. According to the Environmental Defense Fund, "if every American skipped
one meal of chicken per week and substituted vegetables and grains . . .
the carbon dioxide savings would be the same as taking more than half
a million cars off of U.S. roads." Humane Society, "Meatless Mondays,"
http://www.humanesociety.org/assets/pdfs/farm/meatless_mondays_toolkit
_parents.pdf, accessed February 21, 2014.

9. Food and Agriculture Organization of the United Nations (FAO), "Livestock
a major threat to environment: remedies urgently needed," November 29,
2006: http://www.fao.org/newsroom/en/news/2006/1000448/index.html.

10. Makenzi Henderson, "Cow farts may cost ranchers," KOTA-TV, December
11, 2008: http://www.kotatv.com/Global/story.asp?S=9508173&clienttype
=printable.

11. FAO, "Livestock impacts on the environment," November 2006: http://
www.fao.org/ag/magazine/0612sp1.htm.

12. *Human Rights Watch*, "Blood, Sweat, and Fear: Workers' Rights in U.S.
Meat and Poultry Plants," January 25, 2005: http://www.hrw.org/en/reports
/2005/01/24/blood-sweat-and-fear. (Interview with Nebraska Beef meatpacking line worker, Omaha, Nebraska, December 2003, p. 5.)

13. Tory Shepherd, "Slaughterhouse workers are more likely to be violent, study shows," *news.com.au*, January 23, 2013: http://www.news.com.au/national /slaughterhouse-workers-are-more-likely-to-be-violent-study-shows/story -fncynjr2-1226560029984.

14. Ibid.

15. David S. Ludwig, MD, PhD, "Three Daily Servings of Reduced-Fat Milk: An Evidence-Based Recommendation?" *Journal of the American Medical Association Pediatrics*, September 2013: http://archpedi.jamanetwork.com /article.aspx?articleid=1704826.

16. Dr. T. Colin Campbell, *The China Study: The Most Comprehensive Study of Nutrition Ever Conducted* (Dallas, TX: BenBella Books, 2004).

17. Lynda A. Frassetto, Karen M. Todd, R. Curtis Morris, Jr., and Anthony Sebastian, *The Journals of Gerontology Series A*, "Worldwide Incidence of Hip Fracture in Elderly Women: Relation to Consumption of Animal and Vegetable Foods," October 2000: http://biomedgerontology.oxfordjournals .org/content/55/10/M585.abstract.

18. Diane Feskanich, Walter C. Willett, and Graham A. Golditz, "Calcium, vitamin D, milk consumption, and hip fractures: a prospective study among postmenopausal woman," *American Journal of Clinical Nutrition*, February 2003: http://ajcn.nutrition.org/content/77/2/504.full.

Chapter 4: Just Because You're Pro-Choice Doesn't Mean You're Not a Sexist Douche Bag

1. Laura Bassett, *Huffington Post*, August 2013, huffingtonpost.com/2013/08 /26/abortion-clinic-closures_n_3804529.html.

2. Quote from an interview with Foster Friess on MSNBC's *Andrea Mitchell Reports*, February 16, 2012: http://video.msnbc.msn.com/andrea-mitchell /46417914.

3. Charles Jaco, "Jaco Report: Full Interview with Todd Akin," *FOX2now.com*, August 19, 2012: http://fox2now.com/2012/08/19/the-jaco-report-august -19-2012.

4. Diane Greene Foster, Heather Gould, Jessica Taylor, and Tracy A. Weitz, "Attitudes and Decision Making Among Women Seeking Abortions at One U.S. Clinic," *Perspectives on Sexual and Reproductive Health*, 44, no. 2, Guttmacher Institute, June 2012.

5. Laura Ingraham, "The phony war on women," *O'Reilly Factor*, April 9, 2012: http://www.foxnews.com/on-air/oreilly/2012/04/10/laura-ingraham-phony -war-women. *Fox & Friends'* Steve Doocy said he "completely agreed" on

Fox News, April 10, 2012, and Michelle Malkin said the War on Women was "contrived and manufactured" by Democrats to "distract from the economy" on an April 2012 edition of Fox News' *Fox & Friends*. Justin Barrier et al., "Republican 'War on Women' Is Not a Left-Wing Invention," *Media Matters*, April 10, 2012: http://mediamatters.org/research/2012/04/10/republican-war-on-women-is-not-a-left-wing-inve/186151.

6. *The Henry J. Kaiser Family Foundation*, "Kaiser Health Tracking Poll—May 2012," http://kff.org/health-reform/poll-finding/kaiser-health-tracking-poll-may-2012.

7. Kia Makarechi, "CNN's Steubenville Coverage Focuses on Effect Rape Trial Will Have on Rapists, Not Victim," *Huffington Post*, March 17, 2013: http://www.huffingtonpost.com/kia-makarechi/cnn-steubenville-coverage_b_2896948.html.

8. Rebecca Shapiro, "Poppy Harlow, CNN Reporter, 'Outraged' Over Steubenville Rape Coverage Criticism: Report," *Huffington Post*, March 20, 2013: http://www.huffingtonpost.com/2013/03/20/poppy-harlow-cnn-steubenville-rape-coverage-criticism_n_2914853.html.

9. Dave Zirin, "Notre Dame and Penn State: Two Rape Scandals, Only One Cry for Justice," *Nation*, January 7, 2013: http://www.thenation.com/blog/172042/notre-dame-and-penn-state-two-rape-scandals-only-one-cry-justice.

10. *The Raw Story*, "Pat Robertson tells woman to make herself look more attractive to stop 'flirting husband,' June 12, 2010: http://www.rawstory.com/rs/2010/06/12/pat-robertson-tells-woman-attractive-stop.

11. Alex Seitz-Wald, "Pat Robertson's advice to woman whose husband flirts: Make yourself more attractive and 'don't hassle him,'" *ThinkProgress*, June 11, 2010: http://thinkprogress.org/politics/2010/06/11/102133/robertson-advice-wife.

12. Megan Tady, "Women's Bodies, Men's Voices: All-male contraception debates signal rollback of reproductive rights," Fairness & Accuracy in Reporting (FAIR), April 1, 2012: http://fair.org/extra-online-articles/womens-bodies-mens-voices.

13. Faiz Shakir and Adam Peck, "REPORT: By a Nearly 2 to 1 Margin, Cable Networks Call on Men Over Women to Comment on Birth Control," *ThinkProgress*, February 10, 2012: http://thinkprogress.org/media/2012/02/10/423211/cable-report-birth-control-men-women.

14. Curtis Brainard, "Media Hype Swine Flu Report," *Columbia Journalism Review*, August 26, 2009: http://www.cjr.org/the_observatory/media_hypes_swine_flu_report.php?page=all.

15. Rape, Abuse & Incest National Network (RAINN), "97 of Every 100 Rapists Receive No Punishment, RAINN Analysis Shows," http://www.rainn.org /news-room/97-of-every-100-rapists-receive-no-punishment, accessed February 21, 2014.

Chapter 5: The Gay Agenda

1. Gallup poll, "In U.S., 52% Back Law to Legalize Gay Marriage in 50 States," July 29, 2013: http://www.gallup.com/poll/163730/back-law-legalize -gay-marriage-states.aspx.

2. Ben Adler, "How Bryan Fischer Became the Newest Media Darling," *Newsweek*, January 18, 2011: http://www.newsweek.com/how-bryan-fischer -became-newest-media-darling-66841.

3. Sari Horwitz, "Same-sex marriages in Utah legal under federal law, Attorney General Holder says," *Washington Post*, January 10, 2014: http://www .washingtonpost.com/world/national-security/holder-same-sex-marriages-in -utah-legal-under-federal-law/2014/01/10/f08f363a-7a19-11e3-af7f -13bf0e9965f6_story.html.

4. Julie Hollar, "Don't Ask Gays About Don't Ask, Don't Tell: Debate on military policy excludes those most affected," Fairness & Accuracy in Reporting (FAIR), May 1, 2010: http://fair.org/extra-online-articles/dont-ask -gays-about-dont-a sk-dont-tell.

5. Nathaniel Frank, *Unfriendly Fire: How the Gay Ban Undermines the Military and Weakens America* (New York: Thomas Dunne Books, 2009).

6. Michael D. Shear, "As Obama Faces Issues, Domestic and Foreign, an Election Day Test," *New York Times*, September 19, 2010: http://thecaucus .blogs.nytimes.com/2010/09/19/as-obama-faces-issues-domestic-and -foreign-an-election-day-test.

7. Hollar, "Don't Ask Gays About Don't Ask, Don't Tell."

8. Ibid.

9. Human Rights Campaign, "Employment Non-Discrimination Act" (position paper), November 7, 2013: http://www.hrc.org/laws-and-legislation /federal-legislation/employment-non-discrimination-act.

10. Anti-Violence Project (AVP), "Hate Violence Against Lesbian, Gay, Bisexual, Transgender, Quran, and HIV-Affected Communities in the United States in 2011," 2011: www.avp.org/storage/documents/reports/2012_NCAVP _2011_HV-Report.pdf.

11. Madison Park, "Kids who veer from gender norms at higher risk for

abuse," CNN, February 20, 2012: http://www.cnn.com/2012/02/20/health
/child-gender-nonconformity. Lisa Esposito, "Gender Identity Issues Can
Harm Kids' Mental Health: Study," *US News*, February 20, 2012: http://
health.usnews.com/health-news/news/articles/2012/02/20/gender-identity
-issues-can-harm-kids-mental-health-study. Susan Donaldson James,
"Gender-Nonconforming Students at Elevated Risk for Abuse, Post-
Traumatic Stress," *ABC News*, February 20, 2012: http://abcnews.go.com
/Health/gender-nonconforming-students-elevated-risk-abuse-post
-traumatic/story?id=15727672.

12. Richard Herman, *CNN Newsroom*, August 24, 2013; see Carlos Maza,
"CNN Guest Jokes That Chelsea Manning Will Get "Good Practice"
Being a Woman in Prison," August 26, 2013: http://mediamatters.org
/blog/2013/08/26/cnn-guest-jokes-that-chelsea-manning-will-get-g/195605.

13. Christine Haughney, " 'He'? 'She'? News Media Are Encouraged to
Change," *New York Times*, August 22, 2013: http://www.nytimes.com/2013
/08/23/business/media/he-she-news-media-are-encouraged-to-change.html.

14. Margaret Sullivan, "The Soldier Formerly Known as Bradley Manning,"
New York Times, August 22, 2013: http://publiceditor.blogs.nytimes.com
/2013/08/22/the-soldier-formerly-known-as-bradley-manning/?_r=0.

15. Nicole Wallace, *Morning Joe*, MSNBC, August 22, 2013.

16. Joy Reid, "The Manning chat logs: TMI and corroboration of guilt," *Reid
Report Blog*, July 14, 2011: http://blog.reidreport.com/2011/07/manning
-chat-logs/.

17. Mansfield Frazier, "How Will Chelsea Manning Be Treated in Prison?"
Daily Beast, August 22, 2013: http://www.thedailybeast.com/articles/2013
/08/22/how-will-chelsea-manning-be-treated-in-prison.html.

18. Department of Justice 2012 study: "Gay and bisexual prisoners were dis-
proportionately targeted in both men's and women's prisons; a shocking 39
percent of gay male inmates reported being assaulted by other prisoners."

Chapter 6: Fuck the NRA: Guns Don't Kill People; People with Dangerously Underfunded Mental Health Care Programs Do (with Guns)

1. Allison Brennan, "Analysis: Fewer U.S. gun owners own more guns," CNN,
July 31, 2012: http://www.cnn.com/2012/07/31/politics/gun-ownership
-declining/.

2. Megan McArdle, *Daily Beast*, "There's Little We Can Do to Prevent Another Massacre," December 2012, www.thedailybeast/articles/2012/12/17
/there-s-little-we-can-do-to-prevent-another-massacre.html.

3. Steve Almasy and Ashley Fantz, "One piece still missing from puzzle of fatal theater shooting: Why?" CNN, January 14, 2014: http://www.cnn.com/2014/01/14/justice/florida-movie-theater-shooting.

4. *This Week* hosted by George Stephanopoulos, ABC, January 20, 2013.

5. Sean Hannity, *Fox News*, January 18, 2013.

6. "Newtown Answers," *National Review Online*, December 19, 2012: http://www.nationalreview.com/articles/335996/newtown-answers-nro-symposium. "There was not a single adult male on the school premises when the shooting occurred. In this school of 450 students, a sizeable number of whom were undoubtedly 11- and 12-year-old boys (it was a K–6 school), all the personnel—the teachers, the principal, the assistant principal, the school psychologist, the "reading specialist"—were female. There didn't even seem to be a male janitor to heave his bucket at Adam Lanza's knees."

7. Bob Schieffer, *Face the Nation*, CBS, December 16, 2012.

8. Anderson Cooper, *Anderson Cooper 360*, CNN, January 9, 2013.

9. Steve Rendall, "The Self-Defense Self-Delusion: Owning guns doesn't actually help stop gun violence," Fairness & Accuracy in Reporting, March 1, 2013: http://fair.org/extra-online-articles/the-self-defense-self-delusion.

10. Juliet Lapidos, "Defensive Gun Use," *New York Times*, April 15, 2013: http://takingnote.blogs.nytimes.com/2013/04/15/defensive-gun-use/.

11. Danny Hayes, "The media don't care about gun control anymore," *Wonkblog, Washington Post*, December 13, 2013, http://www.washingtonpost.com/blogs/monkey-cage/wp/2013/12/13/the-media-dont-care-about-gun-control-anymore.

Chapter 7: We Know You Smoked Weed in College, Asshole: How the War on Drugs Is Destroying This Country

1. American Civil Liberties Union (ACLU), "A Living Death: Life Without Parole for Nonviolent Offenses," 2013, https://www.aclu.org/files/assets/111813-lwop-complete-report.pdf.

2. Michelle Alexander, *The New Jim Crow: Mass Incarceration in the Age of Colorblindness* (New York: New Press, 2010).

3. Allison Kilkenny, interview with Jack Cole, member of Law Enforcement Against Prohibition (LEAP), May 19, 2009: http://www.huffingtonpost.com/allison-kilkenny/cops-say-to-legalize-drug_b_205112.html.

4. NYCLU, "Stop-and-Frisk Campaign: About the Issue," http://www.nyclu.org/issues/racial-justice/stop-and-frisk-practices, accessed February 21, 2014.

5. *Rolling Stone* interview, 2000.

6. John A. Farrell, "Obama Laughs Off Pot Legalization Talk at Town Hall Meeting," *US News*, March 26, 2009: http://www.usnews.com/opinion /blogs/john-farrell/2009/03/26/obama-laughs-off-pot-legalization-talk-at -town-hall-meeting.

7. Glenn Greenwald, "Drug Decriminalization in Portugal: Lessons for Creating Fair and Successful Drug Policies," CATO Institute, April 2, 2009: http://www.cato.org/publications/white-paper/drug-decriminalization -portugal-lessons-creating-fair-successful-drug-policies.

8. David Remnick, "Going the Distance: On and off the road with Barack Obama," *New Yorker*, January 27, 2014: http://www.newyorker.com/reporting /2014/01/27/140127fa_fact_remnick?currentPage=all.

9. Josmar Trujillo, "Media Laugh Off Criticism of Drug War: Journalists make pot jokes while victims suffer," Fairness & Accuracy in Reporting (FAIR), December 1, 2012: http://fair.org/extra-online-articles/media-laugh-off-criticism -of-drug-war.

10. Ibid.

11. Ibid.

12. Ibid.

13. Allison Kilkenny, "Cops Say to Legalize Drugs," *Huffington Post*, May 2009, www.huffingtonpost.com/allison-kilkenny/cops-say-to-legalize-drug_b_205112 .html.

14. Steve Nelson, "Police Made One Marijuana Arrest Every 42 Seconds in 2012: FBI data: American police made a total of 12,196,959 arrests last year," *US News*, September 16, 2013: http://www.usnews.com/news/articles /2013/09/16/police-made-one-marijuana-arrest-every-42-seconds-in-2012.

15. Kilkenny, "Cops Say to Legalize Drugs."

16. Kristin Cole, "With only 1 medical marijuana dispensary in NJ, Grandma resorts to buying street pot," PIX 11, October 17, 2013: http://pix11.com/2013 /10/17/with-only-1-medical-marijuana-dispensary-in-nj-grandma-resorts -to-buying-street-pot.

17. Kilkenny, interview with LEAP's Jack Cole, 2009.

Chapter 8: USA! USA! USA! We're Here to Help . . . with ~~Drones Cluster Bombs~~ Freedom!

1. Sarah Gilbert, "Peace of the Rock," *New York Post*, March 27, 2003, p. 55.

2. Jenny Eliscu, "War on Protest," *Rolling Stone*, May 1, 2003, p. 9.

3. Spencer Ackerman, "Former NSA chief warns of cyber-terror attacks if Snowden apprehended: Michael Hayden, who also headed the CIA, speculates on global hacker response if Edward Snowden brought back to US," *Guardian*, August 6, 2013: http://www.theguardian.com/technology/2013/aug/06/nsa-director-cyber-terrorism-snowden.

4. Ellen Nakashima and Greg Miller, "U.S. worried about security of files Snowden is thought to have," *Washington Post*, June 24, 2013: http://www.washingtonpost.com/world/national-security/us-officials-worried-about-security-of-files-snowden-is-thought-to-have/2013/06/24/1e036964-dd09-11e2-85de-c03ca84cb4ef_story.html.

5. United Nations' high commissioner for human rights report, March 6, 2013: http://www.ohchr.org/Documents/HRBodies/HRCouncil/RegularSession/Session22/A.HRC.22.35.Add.1_AV.pdf. "During the crisis, 174 Palestinians were killed in Gaza. At least 168 of them were killed by Israeli military action, of whom 101 are believed to be civilians, including 33 children and 13 women. Hundreds of persons were injured. Six civilians, including one woman and three children, may have been killed by rockets fired by Palestinian armed groups that landed in Gaza. In the context of the crisis, six Israelis, including four civilians, were reportedly killed, and 239 Israelis, including 219 civilians, were reportedly injured."

6. Peter Hart, " 'What Palestinians Said Was Israeli Aggression': The Death of Omar al-Masharawi," FAIR, March 12, 2013: http://www.fair.org/blog/2013/03/12/what-palestinians-said-was-israeli-aggression-the-death-of-omar-al-masharawi.

7. Jim Naureckas, "The Strange Thing About Cluster Bombs," FAIR, September 5, 2013: http://www.fair.org/blog/2013/09/05/the-strange-thing-about-cluster-bombs.

8. Rebecca Hellmich, "Who Dies in Yemen Drone Strikes?" FAIR, August 12, 2013: http://www.fair.org/blog/2013/08/12/who-dies-in-yemen-drone-strikes.

9. Jo Becker and Scott Shane, "Secret 'Kill List' Proves a Test of Obama's Principles and Will," *New York Times*, May 29, 2012: http://www.nytimes.com/2012/05/29/world/obamas-leadership-in-war-on-al-qaeda.html?pagewanted=1&_r=2&. "Mr. Obama embraced a disputed method for counting civilian casualties that did little to box him in. It in effect counts all military-age males in a strike zone as combatants, according to several administration officials, unless there is explicit intelligence posthumously proving them innocent."

10. Declan Walsh and Eric Schmitt, "Drone Strike Killed No. 2 in Al Qaeda, U.S. Officials Say," *New York Times*, June 5, 2012:http://www.nytimes.com /2012/06/06/world/asia/qaeda-deputy-killed-in-drone-strike-in-pakistan .html.

11. Peter Hart, "Drone Strike Testimony: Not News?" FAIR, April 24, 2013: http://www.fair.org/blog/2013/04/24/drone-strike-testimony-not-news.

12. Peter Hart, "What's Missing From *Time's* Iran Timeline," FAIR, October 4, 2013: http://www.fair.org/blog/2013/10/04/whats-missing-from-times-iran -timeline.

13. David Nakamura and William Booth, "Israel's Netanyahu warns Obama not to be fooled by Iran's overtures," *Washington Post*, October 1, 2013: http://www .washingtonpost.com/politics/israels-netanyahu-warns-president-obama -not-to-be-fooled-by-irans-overtures/2013/09/30/8660b63c-29db-11e3 -97a3-ff2758228523_print.html.

14. David Brooks, "Defending the Coup," *New York Times*, July 4, 2013: http:// www.nytimes.com/2013/07/05/opinion/brooks-defending-the-coup.html.

15. Nima Shirazi, "Goldberg ignores decades of consistent Iranian statements on nuclear weapons for the sake of propaganda," *Mondoweiss*, October 20, 2012: http://mondoweiss.net/2012/10/goldberg-ignores-decades-of -consistent-iranian-statements-on-nuclear-weapons-for-the-sake-of -propaganda.html.

16. Mike Wallace interview with President Rafsanjani, *60 Minutes*, March 8, 1997: http://www.c-spanvideo.org/program/79946-1.

17. Speech from Supreme Leader Ayatollah Sayyid Ali Khamenei, 2003: http:// islam-pure.de/imam/speeches/speech2003.htm.

18. CNN/Gallup poll, February 19, 2010: http://politicalticker.blogs.cnn .com/2010/02/19/cnn-poll-american-believe-iran-has-nuclear-weapons.

19. *New York Times*/CBS News poll, June 6, 2013: http://www.nytimes.com /interactive/2013/06/06/us/new-york-times-cbs-news-poll-june-2013.html.

Epilogue: Save the Tote Bags!: Why Independent Media Is Essential to Saving Democracy and the World

1. Marcy Wheeler, "Khalid Sheikh Mohammed Was Waterboarded 183 Times in One Month," *Firedoglake*, April 18, 2009: http://emptywheel .firedoglake.com/2009/04/18/khalid-sheikh-mohammed-was-waterboarded -183-times-in-one-month.

2. Alex Wilhelm, "House Republicans Want to Kill Net Neutrality as Part of Their Debt Ceiling Bill," *Techcrunch*, September 26, 2013: http://techcrunch.com/2013/09/26/house-republicans-want-to-kill-net-neutrality-as-part-of-their-debt-ceiling-bill.

3. Matthew Shaer, "In case of Verizon vs. FCC, is net neutrality the real loser?," *Christian Science Monitor*, January 15, 2014: http://www.csmonitor.com/Innovation/2014/0115/In-case-of-Verizon-vs.-FCC-is-net-neutrality-the-real-loser.

4. Sam Gustin, "Net-Neutrality Advocates Angered By FCC's Planned New Rules," *Time*, April 23, 2014, http://time.com/74703/net-neutrality-fcc-rules-plan-angers-advocates/.

5. Pew Research Center, "In Changing News Landscape, Even Television Is Vulnerable: Trends in News Consumption: 1991–2012," September 27, 2012: http://www.people-press.org/2012/09/27/in-changing-news-landscape-even-television-is-vulnerable.

About the Authors

Jamie Kilstein is a stand-up comedian who has been featured on *Conan*, Showtime, *Up with Chris Hayes*, *Countdown with Keith Olbermann*, and NPR's *Weekend Edition*. His latest CD hit number one on iTunes and Amazon. One time, Glenn Beck called him a doofus, which is the nicest thing anyone has ever said to him.

Allison Kilkenny is a former reporter for *The Nation*. She has appeared on MSNBC's *Melissa Harris-Perry Show*, *Up with Chris Hayes*, and *Democracy Now*. One time, G. Gordon Liddy told Allison that her writing "makes him want to vomit," which is the nicest thing anyone has ever said to her.

Visit them and learn more about being awesome at www.wearecitizenradio.com.